The World Wars

Through the Female Gaze

THE WORLD WARS THROUGH THE FEMALE GAZE

Jean Gallagher

SOUTHERN ILLINOIS UNIVERSITY PRESS

CARBONDALE AND EDWARDSVILLE

01 00 99 98   4 3 2 1

Library of Congress Cataloging-in-Publication Data

Gallagher, Jean, 1962–

   The world wars through the female gaze / Jean Gallagher.

     p.   cm.

   Includes bibliographical references and index.

   1. World War, 1914–1918 — Personal narratives, American. 2. World
War, 1914–1918 — Pictorial works. 3. World War, 1939–1945 — Personal narratives,
American. 4. World War, 1939–1945 — Pictorial works. 5. Women — United
States — Biography. 6. Visual perception.

   I. Title.

   D640.A2G35 1998

   940.4′8173 — dc21   97-48874

   ISBN 0-8093-2208-0 (cloth : alk. paper)   CIP

For David S. Birdsell

Contents

Plates

Acknowledgments

My deepest and most enduring debt as a writer, reader, and feminist is to Marie Ponsot; just about every sentence I have written in the past fifteen years owes something to her teaching, conversation, and writing about writing.

Jane Marcus introduced me to women's writing about the world wars and has provided unflagging guidance and enthusiasm at all stages of composition. Her unerring eye also led me to several of the images that appear in this book. My thanks also to William Kelly and Barbara Bowen, who were supportive and encouraging readers of the first draft of this book. Margaret Higonnet and Shari Benstock both generously offered support, encouragement, and suggestions for the project. Barbara Shollar, Patricia Haag, June Bobb, and Delores DeLuise were careful, critical readers of early versions of several chapters. Seth Schein shared his knowledge of Greek drama with me in my early attempts to work on H.D.'s chorus translations.

This book has benefited greatly from the expertise and helpfulness of Carole Callow, the curator of the Lee Miller Archives. Walton Rawls provided a great deal of information on tracking down illustrations for chapter 1.

I am grateful to my colleagues in the Department of Humanities and Social Sciences at Polytechnic University, particularly Richard Wener, for providing the time and support to finish this book. Many of my colleagues there, especially Lou Menashe, Bliss Lim, and David Kilpatrick, were an engaging and critical audience during a presentation of the material in chapter 4.

The Helaine Newstead Dissertation Fellowship at the CUNY Graduate Center made possible a fruitful year of research and writing. The Carolyn G. Heilbrun Dissertation Award in Women's Studies and the Adrienne Munich Dissertation Award from the Ph.D. Program in English at the CUNY Graduate Center provided financial support during the early stages of revising.

Several friends and colleagues heard various versions of chapters at conferences and have consistently offered good talk and great eye contact: Marybeth McMahon, Scott Zaluda, Jane Collins, Lorna Smedman, Danell Jones, Sue Grayzel, Marlowe Miller, and Page Delano. William Boddy, Alison Griffiths, and Bliss Lim pointed me in helpful directions in my readings in film theory.

I am grateful for the many, many gifts, most of which are not countable, given to me by Judy Gallagher. I also thank Sharona Berken, who has been a sustaining friend throughout all my ventures, including this one. David S. Birdsell has been this book's closest reader, sharing with me all the benefits of his ferocious intelligence and a life of ongoing conversation. This book's dedication to him can only hint at the ways he has helped me see.

I extend my thanks to the following for reproduction and reprint permissions: George Dembo, for the reproduction of Frank Brangwyn's poster "Look after My Folks." Gordon and Breach Publishers, for permission to use portions of my previously published article "The Great War and the Female Gaze: Edith Wharton and the Iconography of War Propaganda (*LIT: Literature, Interpretation, Theory* 7 [spring 1996]: 27–49) in chapter 1. The estate of Man Ray, for permission to reproduce photographs by Man Ray. Susan Meyer, for the reproduction of James Montgomery Flagg's poster "Stage Women's War Relief." The Lee Miller Archives, for permission to reproduce Miller's photographs. The Museum of the City of New York, for photographic copies of Neysa McMein's "One of a Thousand YMCA Girls in France" and Frank Brangwyn's "Help Your Country Stop This." Charles Scribner's Sons, for permission to reproduce the photograph of Edith Wharton from *Fighting France*. The estate of Gertrude Stein, for permission to quote from "Mildred Aldrich Saturday." The Yale Collection of American Literature, Beinecke Rare Book Room and Manuscript Library, Yale University, for permission to quote from the typescript of Gertrude Stein's "Mildred Aldrich Saturday" and to reprint the photograph of Gertrude Stein in Berchtesgaden. New Directions Publishing Corporation, for permission to quote from H.D.'s *Within the Walls* and *The Gift* (copyright © 1986, 1988 by Perdita Shaffner. Used by permission of New Directions Publishing Corporation).

The World Wars
Through the Female Gaze

Introduction

I myself have seen the floating ships
And nothing will ever be the same —
The shouts,
The harrowing voices in the house.
I stand apart with an army:
My mind is graven with ships.
　　　— H.D., translation of the "Chorus of the Women of Chalkis,"
　　　　　　　　　from Euripides' *Iphigeneia in Aulis*

The problem of knowing who is the subject of the state and
war will be exactly the same kind as the problem of knowing
who is the subject of perception.
　　　　　　　　— MAURICE MERLEAU-PONTY,
　　　　　　　　　qtd. in Virilio, *War and Cinema*

TO BEGIN THIS STUDY OF GENDER, VISION, AND THE WORLD
wars, I offer two brief parables, one literary and one visual: First, H.D.'s
translations of the Choruses from Euripides' *Iphigeneia in Aulis*, made just
prior to and during World War I, represent a crucial role assigned to women
in writing about war in Western culture. The women at the shoreline
at Aulis are admiring spectators, protesting witnesses, awed and resigned
seeing subjects of a belligerent empire. They are dazzled, puzzled, and
wounded by the sight of the gathering Greek forces:

> If a god should stand here
> He could not speak
> At the sight of ships
> Circled with ships.
> This beauty is too much

> For any woman.
> It is burnt across my eyes.   (*Collected Poems* 73–74)

The women of Chalkis not only actively look at the evidence of impending military action but claim to bear physically the "graven" and "burnt" visible marks of massed military power.

Second, a 1940 photograph taken by Lee Miller for *Vogue* magazine shows two women perched on the edge of a Hampstead bomb shelter, looking toward the photographer and viewer (plate 1). Each wears an elaborate mask or visor, protective eyewear suggested for use during incendiary bombing raids (Penrose 99). Posed for female viewers' visual consumption and identification, these two figures ask us to consider how women were looked at during World War II and how they in turn looked through a set of technological contrivances, the literal and figurative, physical and rhetorical technologies of vision that constrained and constituted how they saw and were seen.

The poem and the photograph suggest the troubled nature of vision for women in a belligerent culture. The women of Chalkis claim the authority to speak as witnesses ("I myself have seen"), but what they see is a potentially damaging excess of visual experience, "too much for any woman." Miller's models seem to look directly toward the viewer, but that direct gaze is mediated by masks designed to protect them from the blinding effects of weapons. Both poem and photograph construe women as active seeing subjects who are at the same time exposed to the dangers of wartime vision. During the two world wars, when Western culture's understanding of what constituted "seeing war" changed drastically due to trench warfare, massive civilian bombardment, and the Holocaust and when the nature of "seeing" itself was under interrogation in philosophical discourse, the construction of the female seeing subject was a vital concern for several women writers and photographers whose work I will be examining in this book.

The study of gender and war—how attention to gender makes us re-envision what we know about war, as well as how war illuminates and recasts the workings of gender—is a field that has recently come into view for feminist scholars in a number of disciplines. Historians, literary critics and theorists, political scientists, and sociologists have begun to analyze the mutual influence of the discourses of war and gender, reflecting Margaret Higonnet's claim that "war must be understood as a gendering activity, one that ritually marks the gender of all members of a society" and that "draws upon preexisting gender definitions at the same time that it restructures gender relations" (4).[1]

Much of this recent work on gender and war has made clear that the wartime experiences of noncombatants provide important material for understanding war and for exploring the intersecting ideologies of war and gender. Vision is one of the crucial elements that has traditionally marked the gendered division of war experience: men "see battle"; women, as noncombatants *par excellence*, do not.[2] However, even as women have often been identified as those who do not see during war, they have at the same time been construed as the primary spectators of war.[3] Susan Schweik observes that traditional war poetry in the West "has enacted its arguments about the nature and meaning of war within scenes of female spectatorship" (90), drawing a clear and gendered distinction between the masculine "authoritative eyewitness" and the feminine "passive spectator" (149–50). Barbara Bowen points out that in many Western narratives, men are punished for *in*active spectatorship of battle, recounting a tale out of Herodotus in which a Thracian king blinds his sons for following their desire to "see the wars" without participating in them (9). Vision has functioned, then, not only as a mark of and basis for authenticity and authority in writing about war but has played an important role in the development and gendering of cultural discourses about war.

Moreover, war has often been understood primarily as something to be seen, a spectacle that "must be *viewed* in order to take place," an understanding evident in the phrase "theater of war" (Bowen 8). Paul Virilio notes that in military theory, an army is often considered the audience or spectator of its opponent's visible military performance: "War can never break free from the magical spectacle because its very purpose is to *produce* that spectacle: to fell the enemy is not so much to capture as to 'captivate' him, to instil the fear of death before he actually dies. . . . There is no war, then, without representation" (5–6). War can, then, be understood in part as a visual activity; vision engenders and genders cultural discourse about war.

The texts that are the focus of this study were produced during a period of intense intellectual ferment concerning the nature and reliability of visual experience. Martin Jay in *Downcast Eyes* has identified this cultural shift as "the denigration of vision" (15) and the development of an "antiocularcentric discourse" (17) in twentieth-century thought. Central to this cultural shift was the late nineteenth century's critique of what Jay calls "Cartesian perspectivalism," Western culture's dominant "scopic regime" since the Renaissance, which posited an unchanging, central, transcendental subject of vision and knowledge (189). Beginning in the late nineteenth century, the primacy of such a model of vision and knowledge — and ultimately the hegemony of vision itself as an organizing principle of human experience — came under increasing attack as a result of a range of social and technological changes (146–47).

Military technology and strategy during the world wars contributed to this antiocularcentric tendency in the twentieth century. Historians and critics have observed a tension or anxiety about the possibility of complete — or any — vision during the world wars, a tension first manifested in the perceptual conflict concerning the "theatricalization" of World War I. While the "theater of war" metaphor appears to have become a staple of popular discourse by the time of World War I (Bowen 4), the theatricalization of war — its visual accessibility to large numbers of military and civilian spectators situated in a privileged viewing position akin to that of the subject of Cartesian perspectivalism — actually reached its peak and began its decline very early in that conflict due to the development of trench warfare. Eric Leed writes that for World War I combatants, "the invisibility of the enemy, and the retirement of troops underground, destroyed any notion that war was a spectacle of contending humanity" (19), and according to Virilio,

> the last romantic battle had long since taken place, in 1914 on the Marne. The war had become a static conflict. . . . To the naked eye, the vast new battlefield seems to be composed of nothing — no more trees or vegetation, no more water or even earth, no hand-to-hand encounters, no visible trace of the unity of homicide and suicide. (15)

In addition to the literal "disappearance" of the war from the sight of combatants, this period saw the development, begun early in World War I and developed extensively in World War II, of "the most sophisticated forms of 'telescopic sight,'" the "eyeless vision" of "optical or opto-electronic processes" in weapons technology (Virilio 69).

This de-theatricalization of war and the development of an immense optical-weapons technology during the world wars suggest that we consider soldiers and civilians during the two world wars not so much as spectators but as *observers* of war. I find particularly useful here Jonathan Crary's distinction between "spectator" (with its connotations of a "passive onlooker at a spectacle") and "observer," which he defines as "one who sees within a prescribed set of possibilities, one who is embedded in a system of conventions and limitations" (5–6).[4] Norman Bryson establishes a parallel set of terms in his discussion of *vision*, the "notion of unmediated visual experience," as distinct from *visuality*, a "cultural construct" or "network of meanings" that make up "the socially agreed[-upon] description(s) of an intelligible world" ("The Gaze" 91–92).

In this book, I read and view texts produced in the first half of the twentieth century by American women who were concerned with visuality, with the processes and contradictions of the act of seeing that was central to their representations of war and gender in the first half of the twentieth century. I am concerned with how the American female observer of the world wars might have been constructed by a belligerent culture's "systems of conventions and limitations" and with how that observer might have resisted such conventions and limitations.

The wartime texts at the center of my study are, like the twentieth-century French intellectuals whom Jay reads, "extraordinarily sensitive to the importance of the visual and no less suspicious of its implications" (*Downcast Eyes* 588). However, I find that the suspicions of these texts are aimed not so much at the visual per se, but rather at one specific model of vision and knowledge, *specularity*. Critical definitions of specularity (and the related concept of "speculation") associate it with the Cartesian model of the subject and invariably employ the metaphor of a mirror to describe a totalized visual field: "a mirror reflecting only itself with no remainder" (Jay, *Downcast Eyes* 31–32) or the eye "seeing itself in an infinite reflection" (Jay, "Scopic Regimes" 64). According to Rodolphe Gasché, specular reasoning and vision "deliberately pursue . . . a totalizing goal" (54):

> The mirroring that constitutes speculative thought articulates the diverse, and the contradictions that exist between its elements, in such a way as to

> exhibit the totality of which this diversity is a part. Speculation, then, is the movement that constitutes the most complete unity, the ultimate foundation of all possible diversity, opposition, and contradiction. (44)

Luce Irigaray has argued that this visual and epistemological tradition of speculation is founded on sexual difference: women, or cultural constructions of women as "woman," have been imagined as the medium, the mirror, that reflects the male gaze seeking its own reflection. According to this theory, "woman" can only exist within this closed visual circuit in Western philosophy, which is "incapable of representing femininity/woman other than as the negative of its *own* reflection" (Moi 132). The scenario is often imagined in terms of entrapment and constraint: women "are imprisoned in a male specular economy in which they are always devalued as inferior versions of the male subject, as mere objects of exchange, dead commodities" (Jay, *Downcast Eyes* 533).

The texts discussed in my study tend to associate specular totality with the workings of militarism (and its extreme extension in fascism) and its attempts to create a unified national subject that will repress or erase any disrupting traces of difference — ideological, sexual, or racial. These texts hold forth and interrogate the promise of complete or totalized visual apprehension of war, and, by association, the unified wartime seeing subject. They offer as well an emerging alternative model of fragmented or indirect visual apprehension, constructing their wartime female observers through failures, gaps, or blockages in vision.

All of the texts I examine were produced by American women living in Europe during the world wars. All address, explicitly or implicitly, an American audience (located in a "neutral" or a belligerent United States) from a site of overt military action or government-organized violence: the French front in 1915, Nazi-occupied Czechoslovakia in 1938, Occupied France 1940–44, Paris immediately following the Liberation, the defeated Germany of 1945, and London under the Blitz. Part 1, "The Great War and the Female Observer: Eyewitness Texts and the Subject of Propaganda," examines two instances of war propaganda, both written by American women in France in 1915, both dedicated to encouraging monetary and military support for the Allied cause against Germany, and both invested in inscribing the female gaze as the basis for writerly authority in an "eyewitness" narrative. Both Edith Wharton's *Fighting France* and Mildred Aldrich's *A Hilltop on the Marne* offer a complex and often contradictory sense of a woman writer's struggles with authority, resistance, the specular, and the promises and impossibilities of "direct" vision of war. These chapters consider the construction of both author and readers as subjects of propaganda and examine how the texts create potential escapes from or alternatives to the sort of militarized subject they attempt to create.

Part 2, "Regarding Fascism," turns to literary and visual texts produced by two female journalists between 1940 and 1945. Chapter 3 is concerned with how Martha Gellhorn's 1940 novel *A Stricken Field* provides a range of gendered seeing positions within, and in opposition to, the visual ideologies of fascism during the Nazi occupation of Czechoslovakia. Chapter 4 looks at Lee Miller's war correspondence and photography for *Vogue* magazine in order to explore how she constructed herself and her predominantly female American audience as antifascist observers of war by working with and against some of the conventions of surrealist and fashion photography.

Part 3 focuses on the experimental autobiographical prose of H.D. and Gertrude Stein in order to explore the functions of vision on two World War II "home fronts": London during the Blitz and Vichy France. Chapter 5 examines how H.D. inscribes an expanded field of vision that privileges several forms of "visual disturbance," such as hallucination, in order to illuminate the relations between wartime visuality and the specular structures of the patriarchal family. In chapter 6, I discuss how Stein's representations of an intensely restricted visual field and her refusal to interpret visual experience during the Nazi occupation of France serve both to advance and to trouble her highly conflicted Vichy-era propaganda.

My project is to map one portion of a historicized, gendered territory—what Nancy K. Miller calls "the gaze in representation" (165). My use of the term "gaze" is meant to convey a number of visual acts within specific historic contexts that help to construct the wartime female subject. It refers both to a female observer's physical act of looking—or refusing to look—at wartime visual objects (a battlefield, a wounded soldier, a torture victim, a national flag, a bombed city, or a wartime hallucination) and to the visual or verbal representation of that act for a reading or viewing audience. This gaze is continually subject to the various forces that constitute wartime visuality and subjectivity and that attempt to direct or constrain the act of looking and the interpretation of visual experience. Some of these forces are human, such as soldiers and police. Some are technological, such as the camera, the telescope, the panorama, or the optical-weapons array. Still other forces at work are discursive and/or ideological: the conventions of war narrative, visual and verbal war propaganda, press regulations concerning what kind of photographs may be published in wartime, and cultural assumptions about what constitutes the "visible."[5]

H.D.'s women of Chalkis, figuring the limits of and effects on the female gaze at the beginning of Western narrative's "originary war" (Bowen 7), claim that "nothing will ever be the same." What I hope to show in this study is the difference six women artists might make to our understanding of the visual cultures of the world wars and how their representations of the wartime gaze ask for our attention to the construction of difference on the wartime visual field.

The Great War
and the
Female Observer:
Eyewitness Texts
and the Subject
of Propaganda

1

Edith Wharton and the Iconography of War Propaganda

The governing principle of the "war narrative" genre is implicit in Hector's admonition to Andromache — "the men must see to the fighting" — namely that women must *not* see to the fighting.
— NANCY HUSTON, "Tales of War and Tears of Women"

It is one of the most detestable things about war that everything connected with it, except the death and ruin that result, is . . . so visually stimulating and absorbing.
— EDITH WHARTON, *Fighting France*

N THIS CHAPTER, I WILL BE LOOKING AT TWO TEXTS BY EDITH Wharton — a 1919 short story called "Writing a War Story" and a 1915 collection of essays, *Fighting France* — in order to explore their inscriptions of vision, gender, and militarism. I am particularly interested in how the acts of seeing, represented in and invited by these two texts, might have worked to construct wartime female subjectivity. While popular discourse during the world wars, such as recruiting posters, has often tended to reinforce women's position as objects of a male gaze,[1] a culture at war also requires that women be inscribed as seeing-subjects in order to enlist their support for military action. My suggestion is that Wharton's work shows how the enlistment of the female gaze — both the gaze of the female characters *within* the texts and the female readers *of* the texts — accomplishes several conflicting things, particularly in relation to the workings of specularity in war. On the one hand, the enlistment of women's vision through writing and reading about war involves them within a wartime specular economy that tightly regulates their positions as subjects and objects of militaristic sight. On the other hand, such an enlistment allows for a potential disruption of that economy, not only allowing for the possibility of a woman's escape from specular military visuality but recasting that visuality as something that traps or contains male soldiers. Examining patterns of specularity and of the regulation of wartime vision in Wharton's works will allow a close look at this process and its deconstruction in a specific historical moment.

Very much at issue in reading these texts is the relation between propaganda and female writerly authority. The *Scribner's* magazine articles collected in *Fighting France* were written in order to raise money in the United States for the work of the Red Cross in France (Buitenhuis 62) and to raise American awareness of and support for the European Allies. One of the aims of war propaganda is to build a unified, collective subject who will then actively support a nation's war-effort.[2] How then can Wharton, as a woman writer of propaganda, construct such a subject if, as Nancy Huston has observed, women have traditionally been the "captive audience" (274) rather than the inventors of war narrative? While women are most often construed by critics and historians as consumers and icons of World War propaganda,[3] Wharton and many of her female contemporaries during World War I wrote propaganda texts that announced (and often problematized) their own status as "eyewitness narratives."[4] The privileged position of "witness" near or on the sites of battle allowed these women to negotiate the discursive and physical space between audience and combatant. In doing so, these writers attempted to establish the often troubled legitimacy of their texts and to address and construct their readers through an appeal to the authority of vision.

Reading "Writing a War Story" alongside of *Fighting France* suggests that the inscription of the wartime female gaze can both exemplify and undermine the workings of specular thought. "Writing a War Story" demonstrates how a woman writer who cannot claim the authority of having "seen" the front is trapped within the extremely narrow confines of wartime specularity. In *Fighting France*, Wharton relies on her position as eyewitness and on a complex and often vexed series of visual strategies to escape and/or reconfigure such confines, to confer authority on her "eyewitness" text, and to mobilize both the female writing and reading subject through sight—a mobilization that has some disrupting effects on the work of propaganda.

"Writing a War Story," written a year after the end of World War I, is a compact and satirical cautionary tale of the discursive constraints placed on women writers during wartime. While it is ostensibly the women writers themselves who are the targets of Wharton's satire, I also want to suggest that it is the specularizing tradition of wartime narrative that also comes up for critique in this story. Through its two models of women writers, this story suggests that when they participate in the discourses of war, women must always be either the mimics of a soldier's voice or pure image, the silent objects of a soldier's desiring gaze. As I hope to show, the pattern of specularity evident in this story reflects how, in Moi's words, "[c]aught in the specular logic of patriarchy, woman can choose either to remain silent, producing incomprehensible babble (any utterance that falls outside the logic of the same will by definition be incomprehensible to the male master discourse), or to *enact* the specular representation of herself as a lesser male" (Moi 135).

In this story, a small-time American poet named Ivy Spang, who has volunteered to pour tea in "a big Anglo-American hospital in Paris" (359), is asked by an editor to write "a good stirring trench story" (360) for the *Man-at-Arms*, a magazine for wounded British soldiers. The editor himself professes a shaky commitment to the principle that the contributors to the issue be authorized eyewitnesses, establishing Ivy as a kind of bad copy, an inferior version of a war eyewitness: "'We want the first number to be an "actuality," as the French say; all the articles written by people who've done the thing themselves, or seen it done. You've been at the front, I suppose? As far as Rheims, once? That's capital!'" (360)

Among the other things that Ivy has never done nor seen done is the writing of fiction; she turns for help to her old French governess, identified only as "Mademoiselle." Mademoiselle is also working in a hospital and tells Ivy that she has transcribed the personal narratives of several wounded French soldiers: "'just as the soldiers told them to me,'" she claims, "'—oh, without any art at all . . . simply for myself, you understand. . . .'" (363; ellipses are Wharton's). The governess's "artless" transcriptions of these stories are recorded in the same notebook as are Mademoiselle's "lecture notes on Mr. Bergson's course at the Sorbonne in 1913" (364). Before appropriating and revising one of these narratives, Ivy notices that it "poured on and on without a paragraph—a good deal like life itself"—and a good deal like Henri Bergson's ideas about what modernist art might accomplish. Bergson theorized of a stream-of-consciousness prose that would restore to readers an awareness of the continuous flux of "direct experience" or "real duration,"[5] which, as we will see, is an ideal that this story both establishes and dismantles.

However, there is another element of Bergson's philosophy that has a bearing on Wharton's representations of gendered wartime visuality. According to Jay, Bergson's work provided "the initial frontal attack on ocularcentrism in modern French philosophy" (*Downcast Eyes* 186). For Jay, Bergson's critique of the centrality of sight (especially of the visual and epistemological model posited by Cartesian perspectivalism) was grounded on three premises: "the detranscendentalization of perspective," "the recorporealization of the cognitive subject," and the "revalorization of time over space" (187). The first and second of these premises in particular are relevant to my reading of Wharton's representation of the female subject and object of vision during World War I. According to Jay, Bergson's critique of ocularcentrism was based on a privileging of the role of the body in perception; the body was "the ground of our acting in the world" rather than "merely one of innumerable 'things' in the material world" to be seen and analyzed (Jay 192–93). As we will find, the specifically female body as an object of soldierly and self-contemplation in "Writing a War Story" both contrasts with and complements Wharton's own self-representation as an eyewitness in *Fighting France*.

One effect of the traces of the Bergson lecture in "Writing a War Story" is to hold out the possibility of a "natural," transparent war-writing that would accomplish the modernist ideal of articulating immediate experience. The soldier's story is posited as free from narrative conventions, making male military experience the source of immediate, "real" narratives that women may only mimic. However, neither this "artless" direct transcription nor any part of the Bergson lectures are directly quoted in the story. The absence of the "real story," the unfulfilled promise of a narrative that will deliver directly the soldier's experience of war, reflects a problem recognized by many writers during and since the World War I period: the difficulties or impossibilities of "realistic" mimetic language. This problem is expressed in a particularly troubled and troubling way by Henry James, who said in a 1915 interview, "The war has used up words. . . . they have . . . been more overstrained and knocked about and voided of the happy semblance during the last six months than in all the long ages before" (qtd. in Buitenhuis 59). The phrase "voided of the happy semblance" and the absence of any indirect object or term of comparison following it (semblance of what?) underlines and enacts in language the gap in mimesis that so much concerned James, Wharton, and their contemporaries during and after the war.[6]

However, in "Writing a War Story," it would appear that miming male voices is the only possible choice for Ivy and Mademoiselle, even as they seek to avoid it. In rewriting the soldier's narrative in order to avoid "artless" transcription, Ivy and her coauthor end up imitating older literary conventions and styles. The final product of this collaboration, according to the narrator, reflects outdated models of how women have conventionally spoken about war: "it finally issued forth in the language that a young lady writing a composition of the battle of Hastings would have used in Mademoiselle's school days" (364). The women writing a war story are placed between two possible poles of mimesis: the soldier's transcribed voice and nineteenth-century rhetorical traditions of representing war. The restraints on Ivy and Mademoiselle's narrative and the textual repression of any "genuine" or "natural" or "direct" representation of war suggests that mimicry constitutes the only writerly ground for these women writing about the war. While Nancy Huston claims that "war imitates war narrative imitating war" (273), it would appear that for the women writers in Wharton's story, war narrative imitates war narrative imitating war narrative.

When Ivy's story is published and distributed to wounded soldiers in her hospital, her concern is that it resemble a soldier's experience as closely as possible. She asks a group of soldiers she finds reading the *Man-at-Arms* to "open at the first page of her story," " 'You think it's really like, do you?' " (367). Similar to Henry James's phrase "happy semblance," the phrase "really like," missing the second term of the comparison, both emphasizes and undermines wartime language's mimetic possibilities.

The soldiers' answer to Ivy's question, however, shifts the terms of mimesis from verbal to visual and from the woman as a writing subject (or a mimicked version of a writing subject) to the woman's reproduced image as the object of the male desiring gaze. The soldiers answer, "Really like? Rather!" (367), but they are not reading Ivy's story. They are instead looking at the photograph of her in a nurse's uniform that accompanies her text. The proofs of this photo arriving in the mail had, several pages earlier in the story, convinced the beleaguered Ivy to continue her "battle with the art of fiction": "she saw herself, exceedingly long, narrow and sinuous, robed in white and monastically veiled, holding out a refreshing beverage to an invisible sufferer. . . . The photograph was really too charming to be wasted" (364).

The image of Ivy described here is similar to many found in the iconography of Great War posters and combines the elements of two well-known American posters. The first is a 1918 Y.M.C.A. War Work Campaign poster that features a woman in dark clothes, apparently a uniform that includes a sober hat and tie (plate 2). She is holding out a steaming cup in one hand and holding two books in the other. The second poster, designed for an organization called the Stage Women's War Relief, represents the kind of long, narrow, sinuous, white-robed and -veiled image that Ivy sees in her photograph (plate 3). The figure in this second poster, however, holding out an empty hand, is in the act of doffing a voluminous fur-trimmed coat, and the frame around the figure roughly represents a proscenium arch and footlights. The framing of this figure of the nurse (first by the stage apparatus and then by the fur coat) suggests several concentric circles of mimesis: the drawing of a female figure representing an actress representing a socialite dressed as a nurse.

Looking at these two posters side by side enables a viewer to rough out a part of World War I iconography of women caregivers, an iconography that Wharton's story reproduces and parodies. Within the logic of "Writing a War Story," the woman writer who has no access to the visual authority of having seen a war zone (not to mention access to writerly talent) is bound to occupy a different position on the spectrum of wartime visuality: as the object, rather than the subject, of sight, and as a part of wartime iconography of the female body. Ivy's image becomes the pictorial commodity that the soldiers would like to carry away as part of a war souvenir: They ask her "'to give one to each of us . . . to frame and take away with us. . . . There's a chap here who makes rather jolly frames out of Vichy corks'" (367).

The "framing" of Ivy's photograph as part of the popular iconography of nurses during the Great War is continued and intensified by the wounded male novelist in the ward who, unlike the other soldiers, does read (and then laughs at) Ivy's story. Then, like the soldiers, he asks for a copy of the photograph. The novelist suggests that if women are to participate at all in writing about war, they must limit themselves to a stricter miming of male narrative. He tells Ivy, "you've got hold of an awfully good subject, . . . but you've rather mauled it, haven't you?" (369). The novelist's critique of Ivy's story quickly shifts to a critique of Ivy herself, positioning her as an object of a male gaze and thereby as an object of male narrative: "You were angry just now because I didn't admire your story; and now you're angrier still because I do admire your photograph. Do you wonder that we novelists find such an inexhaustible field in Woman?" (370). The novelist's words situate Ivy grammatically as the object of his specularizing "admiration" and narration. The extremely narrow range of positions open to Ivy as a subject and object of representation reflects Moi's claim that within specular thought, "[t]he thinking man not only projects his desire for a reproduction of himself (for his own reflection) on to the woman; he is . . . incapable of *thinking* outside this specular structure" (133).

In "Writing a War Story," the parameters that define women writers' relationship to representation in wartime — mimicking a soldier's voice or becoming the fixed visual object of the desiring male gaze (and of male narrative) — mark women's (and women writers') frozen positions in the specular discourses of war. For Wharton, becoming an eyewitness at the French front holds out the possibility for a woman writer to position herself outside of these boundaries and to mobilize her gaze and her own writerly authority — in Bergsonian terms, to posit her body as the ground of perception rather than an object of contemplation. However, that act of eyewitnessing also opens up new avenues of specular entrapment for the female observer as well as new avenues of resistance to that entrapment.

Wharton's 1915 essays, written for *Scribner's* magazine and collected later that year as *Fighting France*, feature a remarkable verbal attempt to represent the visual experience of touring the battle front: "the look" of mobilized France and the complex acts of politicized seeing. In its inscriptions of her own acts of seeing, Wharton's text suggests that in war, the specular's relation to sexual difference might be reconfigured as something between men, a homosocial visuality that situates the female observer outside of its circle. That war is often understood as a male homosocial construct, which is certainly not a new idea; what interests me is how Wharton's text represents that structure in terms of vision and specularity, how she positions the female observer in relation to it, and how this positioning tends to disrupt the work of her text as war propaganda.

The attention to visual experience in this verbal propaganda text is vital to the construction of politically militarized subjects both inside and outside the text. As the eye is crucial to the construction of the "I" in so much of Western culture's metaphor-making,[7] the eye in Wharton's propaganda text is instrumental in the construction of the collectivized subject, the mobilized "I" that participates in the military policies of a national "we." However, as I suggested earlier, the induction of the seeing female subject as eyewitness-writer and as reader can disrupt the unified subjectivity that war propaganda aims to develop; a gendered gaze disrupts as well as authorizes a woman's eyewitness propaganda text.

In the collection's opening essay, "The Look of Paris," the war exists first as language. Wharton hears verbal "war-rumours" and then sees nailed to a wall France's written declaration of mobilization. The work of this first essay is to attempt to make a verbally understood war visible, to convert it into image and thereby to convert its American readers to supporting the Allied war effort. Describing the spectacle of the newly mobilized soldiers in the streets, Wharton claims, "In an instant we were being shown what mobilization was" (9). The collection as a whole aims to show its readers just such a vision and to induct them into its "we."

Wharton's textual attention to the visual reflects the long cultural tradition, observed by theorists such as W. J. T. Mitchell, Wendy Steiner, and Teresa deLauretis, which privileges images as "immediate, natural, directly linked to reality" over an arbitrary, "artificial" language (deLauretis 10). This contrast between word and image is, as Mitchell observes, often construed in military terms, as "the war for the representation of reality" (*Iconology* 121).[8] However, the most prominent propaganda texts of the Great War—war posters—combine image and text, controlling as many sign-systems as possible in an effort to put together and direct a unified national audience.[9] Wharton's text enters the battle for America's material and military commitment in the European war by attempting to strike a similar truce in the war between word and image.

The terms of this truce between the visual and verbal rest rather uneasily in *Fighting France* on the kind of sign that C. S. Peirce identifies as an index, a sign that gestures towards its object (such as a finger pointing or a demonstrative pronoun) or that bears physical traces of its referent (such as a footprint).[10] According to Rosalind Krauss, "[i]ndexes establish their meaning along the axis of a physical relationship to their referents" (*The Originality of the Avant-Garde* 198). Verbal and physical gestures of *pointing toward* are ubiquitous in *Fighting France*. Almost everything that Wharton witnesses in mobilized France is ultimately an index of, a verbal or visual gesture towards, an unnamed and shifting transcendental signifier of war itself, an always deferred picturing of an always unwritable narrative. At first, this elusive ultimate referent is the political or diplomatic causes of the war (i.e., the perfidy of Germany), indicated only by demonstrative pronouns in French and English: "every one was declaring all over the country . . . '*Il faut que cela finisse!*' 'This kind of thing has got to stop': that was the only phrase one heard" (7). This unnamed referent shifts very quickly to the most unpicturable act of war itself, the unnamed wounding and destruction of bodies that Wharton refers to as "what one dare not picture" (50), and that, as Elaine Scarry points out, is the "main purpose and outcome of war" even though this fact can and does "disappear from view along many separate paths" (63–64).

Wharton's textual indexes are constructed so as to direct and control as far as possible her American readers' gaze and to evoke for them the narratives of wounding that are not directly represented but that readers must imagine in order to support the Allies in Europe. An example of this would be Wharton's description of Parisians looking at the first captured German flag: "they stood and looked at it . . . in silence: as if already foreseeing all it would cost to keep that flag. . . . All day the crowd renewed itself, and it was always the same crowd . . . who looked steadily at the flag and knew what its being there meant. That, in August, was the look of Paris" (28–29). This passage directs the reader's gaze into a dense visual and conceptual network. The Parisians look at the flag, which in turn evokes relative clauses ("all it would cost"; "what its being there meant"), which in turn are indexes of the battle stories that are not articulated here. These images and indexes all attempt indirectly to construct and control the narratives that readers will use to tell themselves about the war, demonstrating in a verbal text what Mitchell claims for visual texts: "what pictorial expression amounts to is the artful planting of certain clues in a picture that allows us to perform an act of ventriloquism" (*Iconology* 41). By channeling the readers' gaze toward the front and toward the collective, uniform "look of Paris" and of Parisians, Wharton's text attempts to control and to mobilize for war virtually the whole field of readerly vision—while holding invisible the central fact of war's wounding.

The text contains several more examples of a verbal indexing that both gestures towards and conceals the visual perception of physical wounding. Viewing a town that has become the headquarters of an army, Wharton writes,

> once the eye has adapted itself to the ugly lines and the neutral tints of the new warfare, the scene . . . becomes positively brilliant. It is a vision of one of the central functions of a great war, in all its concentrated energy, without the saddening suggestions of what, on the distant periphery, that energy is daily and hourly resulting in. (49)

Again, the "what" functions in Wharton's sentence as a verbal index, a gesture toward the "distant periphery" where war's central act of bodily damaging takes place. In another move in this chapter that takes the text both further toward and away from "what" is on that distant periphery, Wharton represents the troubled intersection of civilian and soldierly vision as she describes the soldiers arriving in the town from the front: "it is a grim sight to watch them limping by, and to meet the dazed stare of eyes that have seen what one dare not picture" (50). The observer's encounter with the soldiers' eyes is one of visual displacement and disjuncture rather than of a mutual look. The traces of the soldiers' hidden visual experience reside in their very act of looking without seeming to see, the "dazed stare" that constitutes the object of the civilian gaze.

I suggest that what Wharton's text is doing here is representing the specular structure of military vision: the soldiers engage not in a mutual look but in a kind of internal circuit of vision, seeing neither the eyes of the female civilian observer nor their own reflection in her eyes. Instead, the soldiers are caught in a kind of visual lag, seeing their own past acts of vision, what the text refuses to picture, the visual scene from which Wharton removes herself and readers. This outsider's glimpse of the soldiers' acts of internalized seeing recall Jay's definition of specular thought already quoted in my introduction: "[i]n specular thought, vision is understood not in terms of an eye seeing an object exterior to itself, but rather of the eye seeing itself in an infinite reflection" ("Scopic Regimes" 64). As I will discuss later in the chapter, this brief scene prefigures a later encounter in the text between Wharton and soldierly vision, one in which it becomes clear that the nature of specularity in war positions the female observer outside of its circle and finally undoes the work of indexing upon which so much of the text's propagandistic work relies.

Like "Writing a War Story," *Fighting France*, with its recurring textual indexes, invokes a part of the iconography frequently found in World War I posters. While the gesture or pointing receives its most well-known treatment in the United States in the recruiting posters featuring Uncle Sam, the image that most resembles Wharton's authorial gesture is found in two posters by Frank Brangwyn. In "Help Your Country Stop This" (plate 4), a sailor in a crowded lifeboat in the foreground looks out at the viewer while pointing toward the dark background, where a few darker diagonal bars and smudges suggest a sinking ship. In "Look after My Folks" (plate 5), another sailor on the deck of a sinking ship looks out at the viewer while pointing backwards toward what appears to be smoke. Similar to Wharton's textual indexes, these posters gesture toward unpictured and unidentified acts of destruction, compelling the viewers to fill in the battle narratives signaled only by smudges of black ink and the demonstrative pronoun "this." If "Writing a War Story" inscribes some of the popular wartime iconography of the female figure in order to indicate how it positions women within a wartime visual economy as objects of a specularizing male gaze, the iconography invoked by the indices in *Fighting France* underlines the authority of the writer. It positions the female author, like the pointing sailor, in the space between the civilian viewer or reader and the virtually invisible physical disaster of the war, directing the reader's or viewer's sight and political loyalties.

This act of pointing seems inherently contradictory or conflicted; it draws the reader/viewer's attention both toward and away from the body that gestures and the body of the viewer/reader. Art historians examining visual and verbal indexes offer conflicting ideas about them, particularly about the significance and presence of the body of the gesturer. For Claude Gandelman, the "gesture of demonstration" signals the relative unimportance of the designator; it is an attempt at directing the viewer's gaze elsewhere and rendering "invisible" the one who points, focusing instead on the *viewer's* proximity to the object of vision (127). Bryson, examining the larger visual/verbal structure of deixis (which includes visual and verbal indexes), defines it as "utterances that contain information concerning the locus of utterance" (*Vision and Painting* 87). Deixis "not only describes completed action, but adds a comment from the speaker's own perspective":

> The wider class of deixis therefore includes all those particles and forms of speech where the utterance incorporates into itself information about its own spatial position relative to its content (here, there, near, far off), and its own relative temporality (yesterday, today, tomorrow . . .). Deixis is utterance in carnal form and points back directly . . . to the body of the speaker. (*Vision and Painting* 88)

Another version of the mediating and directive gesture of the index, and one that underlines the problematic status of the female body as the subject and object of vision in wartime, is found in the frontispiece of *Fighting France*: a portrait of Wharton herself in front of a French palisade (plate 6). Like the pointing sailors, Wharton occupies the foreground, the space between the viewer and the unseen war hidden behind the palisade. However, the viewer's gaze is directed toward the invisible war not by any gesture of Wharton's but by the imagined gazes of the two soldiers behind Wharton, as they look out over the front from an observation post with their backs to the viewer. The photograph with its divergent looks is emblematic of the conflicting visual models in *Fighting France*, reflecting Nancy K. Miller's claim that "the gaze is not simply an act of vision, but a site of crisscrossing meanings in which the effects of power relations are . . . displayed" (164). The photograph offers several possible versions of the power relations that govern Wharton, the reader, and the militaristic discourses of the Great War, here visually represented by the soldiers. By sharing the frame with the soldiers, Wharton can at least potentially share the visual experience and authority of the soldiers and see what the viewer cannot. Acting as a mediator between civilian and military sight, she can vouchsafe their—and by extension, her own—visual authority. However, Wharton is also posed with her glance going elsewhere, away from the soldiers, away from the front, engaged instead in a potential mutual look with the photograph's viewer and the text's reader. It is the issue of *Fighting France*'s errant looks—and the text's attempts to contain them—that I now want to explore through several passages that enact the range of wartime visual power relations emblematized by the photograph and that demonstrate how this text's verbal indexes help to put those power relations into play.

As Wharton tours the front lines, the shifting signified, the elusive object of her straining vision becomes the invisible enemy soldiers hidden in a rural landscape, a phenomenon that, Eric Leed has noted, was a central perceptual experience for soldiers in the trenches during the war. Leed suggests that for soldiers at the front, "[t]he invisibility of the enemy put a premium upon auditory signals and seemed to make the war experience peculiarly subjective and intangible" (19). However, it is not only the threatening and disorienting invisibility of the hidden enemy that marks Wharton's visual experience here; her look at the enemy is intensely regulated by the gestures of her soldier-guides:

> Nothing but the wreck of the bridge showed that we were on the edge of war. . . . But there the Germans were. . . . The longer one looked, the more oppressive and menacing the invisibility of the foe became. "*There* they are—and *there*—and *there*." We strained our eyes obediently, but saw only calm hillsides, dozing farms. . . . Suddenly an officer, pointing to the west . . . said: "Do you see that farm? . . . *They are there*." . . . and the innocent vignette framed by my field-glass suddenly glared back at me like a human mask of hate. The loudest cannonade had not made "them" seem as real as that! (109–11)

Here, not only is Wharton's gaze directed by the soldiers, her visual experience is itself constituted by the soldiers' repeated and emphatic verbal and physical pointing, which functions as a far more effective technology of vision than the field glasses themselves. While what Wharton sees does not change, the soldiers' insistent gestures toward the invisible enemy are what renders that enemy real for both the author and the audience of this text, because in actuality both Wharton and the soldiers share the same inability to see. Wharton and her readers must then rely not on her eyewitness experience but on the visual knowledge and physical gestures of the soldiers, which "frame" the visual field for militaristic purposes. Wharton as eyewitness here mediates between seeing and not seeing, between military and civilian sight, straining her eyes obediently and submitting her gaze to military construction—and asking her readers to do the same. At stake in this passage is the very construction of wartime vision and of the wartime female observer. The passage quoted above allows a glimpse of the soldier's very act of prescribing for the female observer and her readers the possibilities of seeing in war's landscape.

Within the framing or construction of militarized vision and the militarized observer, the citizens of a mobilized nation, the inscribed subjects of war propaganda, all look the same. They are seen as similar by the eyes of the propagandist ("It was always the same crowd"), and they all gaze on the same object (the captured flag, the invisible enemy). In an attempt to create politically unified subjects, both within and outside the text, Wharton looks to the faces of soldiers, refugees, and civilians, who not only function as indexes of unwritten battle stories but who bear the visible traces of the totalizing effects of war propaganda itself. Like the civilians gazing at the flag, the most important feature of the soldiers near the front is their sameness, which acts as an index of their battle experience and the values that experience engenders: "Almost all of the faces have the same look . . . as though all . . . fussiness, little personal oddities, meannesses and vulgarities, had been burnt away in a great flame of self-dedication" (54).

Civilian women also act as indexes of the unifying effects of wartime discourse—and as potential models for Wharton's American female readers—but women also signal the earliest place in the text where war's discourse shows the potential for a disrupting difference of vision. Wharton writes that

> Personal sorrow is the sentiment the least visible in the look of Paris. . . .
> I often pass in the street women whose faces look like memorial medals—

idealized images of what they were in the flesh. . . . But none of these faces reveals a personal preoccupation: they are looking, one and all, at France erect on her borders. Even the women who are comparing different widths of Valenciennes at the lace-counter all have something of that vision in their eyes — or else one does not see the ones who haven't. (39)

This passage situates civilian women as both subjects and objects within the intensely specular visual economy of a nation at war, an economy that traffics in endless reflections of the same. As objects of sight, these women themselves are indexes and traces of war and its discourses. Memorial medals, usually the indexes of battle and battle stories, are here also indexes of the workings of war propaganda itself, whose function is to erase from the circuits of a collective war vision all personal desires and griefs and to reinscribe the very bodies of civilians with the marks of a unified national subjectivity. Like the soldiers, these civilian women are mobilized into a visual immobility. As seeing subjects, as militarized observers, their gaze is directed by the unifying discourse of war: all the women in Paris look at the same imagined and imaginary object, "France erect on her borders." The women who do not participate in this mobilized and immobilized gaze are invisible. Like personal sorrow, they do not circulate within the economy of wartime vision or in Wharton's essay. And yet the trace of these invisible women whose gaze is directed elsewhere is, like the unpicturable act of wounding and the hidden presence of the German soldiers, figured in the text by their very invisibility, a potentially threatening gap in the closed circuit of vision that propaganda attempts to create. While the invisible soldiers physically threaten the author, and potentially the readers, of this text, thereby requiring the uniform belligerent gaze of a mobilized nation, the errant look of invisible women threatens the continuity and commitments of the text itself.

Wharton's final trip to the front offers an unsettling vision of how the perfection of a unified wartime gaze allows for its own disruption. Wharton looks over No Man's Land from a hidden observation post that allows a view of both the French and German lines. Seeing the "orderly and untroubled" activities of French soldiers only a few yards from a German trench, she says, "it was one of those strange and contradictory scenes of war that brings home to the bewildered on-looker the utter impossibility of picturing how the thing *really happens*" (208–9; emphasis Wharton's).

Here, the juxtaposition of almost domestic activities and the potential for wounding begins to refract the unified writerly gaze that Wharton has tried to maintain as the writing subject of propaganda. The impossibility of picturing, the absence of any index toward an unpictured image, suggests that her status as eyewitness cannot always evoke the necessary narrative the civilian needs to tell herself in order to support the war. Moreover, this kind of bewilderment was a crucial part of soldiers' perceptual dilemmas at the front. Leed describes "the struggle to fit expectations into the actuality of war . . . ending in incomprehension for many combatants" (132) and claims that

> the war became meaningless for many participants in individual terms. . . . this process was not merely a change of attitude but a function of the transformation of perspective and consciousness necessitated by the realities of war. The very first impression of the war was, for many, an acknowledgment of the peculiar incongruity between its meaning and its actuality. (131–32)

Several sentences after Wharton's confession of visual incomprehension, she describes walking through a long covered observation trench close to the front lines, passing a series of "helmeted watchers" and finally emerging in "a half-ruined farm-house" containing more watchers seated on high shelves. From this "last outpost" (214), only a few yards away from the frontline trenches, Wharton's text shows that the specular circuit of war itself finally freezes men as well as women, soldiers as well as civilians, in its fixed gaze:

> Over a break in the walls I saw another gutted farmhouse close by in another orchard: it was an enemy outpost, and silent watchers in helmets of another shape sat there watching on the same high shelves. . . . I could not understand where we were, or what it was all about. . . . And then, little by little, there came over me the sense of that mute reciprocal watching from trenches to trench: the interlocked stare of innumerable pairs of eyes, stretching on, mile after mile, along the whole sleepless line from Dunkerque to Belfort. (215–16)

Wharton's final vision at the front troubles her text and its commitments in several ways. Once again, her visual experience parallels that of trench soldiers, but her position as a female civilian observer also creates a very different visual field than the one in which soldiers participated. Leed writes that for World War I combatants, "The sudden appearance of the human enemy from behind the mask of technological violence produced a feeling of the . . . uncanny" (20). Wharton's vision grants, at least potentially, to the once invisible, unreadable enemies an uncanny subjectivity equal to that of the French soldiers; the German soldiers are granted this uncanny subjectivity not only because they are seen but because they can see in return. However, the soldiers' subjectivity on both sides of No Man's Land is virtually nullified by the immobilizing exigencies of belligerent sight. Wharton's vision shows how the uniform, (im)mobilized gaze that war propaganda tries to construct finally only mirrors itself, fixing soldiers in a terrifyingly perfect specularity. The final fixed object of the soldierly gaze is the Other-as-mirror, but in this instant of unbroken mirroring, that Other is the military and militarized male. The intensification of specularity in war here turns on itself, rendering men as objects in a mutual gaze through the perception of the female spectator who cannot break the deadly, objectifying look of war but who can make it visible to the reader.

Wharton's verbally rendered image of the "whole sleepless line" recalls the job done by military aerial photography or "macrophotography" during World War I. According to Virilio, military observation photographs and films consisted of a series of "successive negatives" that could analyze "the phases of the movement in question." The goal of such photography was

> to reconstitute the fracture lines of the trenches, to fix the infinite fragmentations of a mined landscape. . . . Thus, as the Hachette *Almanach* of 1916 put it, the techniques of representation proved their enormous importance during the war: "Thanks to the negatives and films, it was possible to retrace the whole front with the greatest clarity, from Belfort to the Yser." (70–71)

Leed notes that the imagined aerial view was one of the perceptual and imaginative survival strategies used by trench-bound soldiers: their visual "disorientation . . . generated a need for a coherent vision, the kind of vision attributed to the flier, the pilot who enjoyed an aerial perspective" (123). Again, Wharton's visual experience both parallels and differs from that of the soldiers. Attempting to counter her sense of disorientation at the uncanny vision not just of the enemy but of the enemy looking back, she attempts to reconstruct the "look" of the whole front in one imagined sweeping human glance, but her look encounters a frozen repetition of the same image of mutual looking. The constantly disintegrating landscape of trench warfare is fixed, and in reconstituting with her imagined gaze the "fracture lines" of the front, Wharton creates yet another fracture: between herself and the visual confrontation that she sees. Wharton's vision of her own visual isolation at the front, outside the fixity of the soldiers' gaze, threatens her subject position as war's seeing eye. The infinite regress of sight at the very center of the war locates and then stops visual perception at the mirror that is No Man's Land. The war itself becomes a function of the mutual, belligerent male gaze, the mirroring, fixed vision of soldiers, an absolutely closed circuit of sight that excludes the gaze of the female observer.

As we have seen with the invisible women of Paris, to refuse to participate in war vision, to look elsewhere, is to become invisible, is not to exist, except as the disruptive trace in the war's totalizing discourses. All along the line, Wharton has been looking for and pointing toward the images that will support her own text as it supports the Allied military cause — but they vanish from sight. While Wharton's war writing shows the female gaze and the female body as subjects and objects of militarized, specular vision, it is also possible for her essays — and their readers — to recuperate vision for a critique of war and of the unified subjects of war propaganda. Far from the traditions of pacifist women and of suffragists who reappropriated sight and image for antiwar and other-than-war purposes in the early twentieth century,[11] Wharton's final vision at the front does allow for the possibility of making visible another position from which to see the war — the position of its invisible women, looking elsewhere and looking differently.

2

Mapping the
Female Observer in
A Hilltop on the Marne

Not exactly the same as any one can see war and more not exactly the same as any one can see.
— GERTRUDE STEIN, "Mildred Aldrich Saturday"

 WILL BE EXPLORING HERE THE DYNAMICS OF VISION, GEN-
der, and World War I militaristic discourse in Mildred Aldrich's 1915 best
seller, *A Hilltop on the Marne*. As in my reading of *Fighting France*, I am
concerned here with how the female civilian "eyewitness" narrator of this
text is transformed into a militarized observer on the field of vision during
the Great War and with how the gaze of the female observer is a crucial
site both for women's participation in and resistance to the militaristic discourses of the Great War period. Through its narrative and visual elements,
A Hilltop on the Marne maps a set of possibilities for vision during wartime for the female observer and her readers, even as the militaristic discourse that she encounters works to identify her as a passive spectator of the
Battle of the Marne.

As we have already seen in the introduction, Virilio identifies the
Battle of the Marne as "the last romantic battle" of twentieth-century war-

fare. However, he makes clear that this particular battle also provided the first use of aerial reconnaissance in the war (17), thereby becoming the site of considerable perceptual conflict among the French generals, a "conflict of interpretation" between the view of the enemy afforded by aerial reconnaissance and by ground patrols:

> the French high command refused to accept the evidence and quite naturally set greater store by the horizontal, perspectival vision than by the vertical, panoramic vision of overflying aircraft. Eventually Gallieni imposed his "point of view" [that of aerial reconnaissance] on enemy movements. . . . [I]t seems at least plausible that the [victory] . . . depended upon *regulation of points of view*—that is, on a definition of the battle image in which the cavalry's perspective suddenly lost out to the perpendicular vision of the reconnaissance aircraft. (73)

This chapter explores how Aldrich represents a similar "conflict of interpretation" for the female civilian observer during and after the Battle of the Marne and how French military personnel attempt to regulate the female civilian's point of view.

Aldrich was an American journalist who lived in Paris from the turn of the century until she retired in the summer of 1914 to a house about thirty miles north of Paris overlooking the Marne Valley. *A Hilltop on the Marne* is the first of four volumes of letters written from this house to an unnamed correspondent. The letters are based on Aldrich's letters to Gertrude Stein and Alice B. Toklas during and after World War I.[1] In 1922, Aldrich was awarded the Medal of the Legion of Honor by the French government "for helping to sway American opinion toward entrance into World War One" with these volumes (Townsend 37).

The central visual trope in *A Hilltop on the Marne* and the one that works most to create Aldrich as an observer of the war is what Aldrich calls throughout her letters her "panorama," the view of the surrounding Marne valley that she has from her front lawn. I want to take a moment here to discuss the panorama as a popular art form and as a means for constructing subjectivity before exploring it as a model for or parallel of the panorama in Aldrich's text. One type of panorama, extremely popular in the late eighteenth and nineteenth centuries in Europe and in the United States, consisted of a painting executed on the inside of a sphere surrounding a central viewing platform (Lawson 88–89). The most popular subject of these panoramas was the depiction of battles.[2] As Thomas Lawson points out, a panorama privileges the illusion of an "all-seeing" eye (89), hinting at the visual utopia of *seeing everything*.[3]

A battle panorama, then, promises the civilian observer the ability to see war from a central, military, and therefore "true" vantage point. This would have been a particularly seductive promise during the early years of the European war for Aldrich's American readers, a group particularly open to anxiety about authentic vision of war. Rigid press restrictions enforced by the belligerent governments kept journalists and photographers away from the front lines, and American newspaper and film audiences did not find the "authentic" pictures of trench combat that they eagerly sought (Mould 48–65). They did, however, find pictures. Before the entrance of U.S. forces into the European War in 1917, the American press produced a remarkable number of pictorial issues of journals and periodic "albums" of war photographs, which like most of the newsreel footage of 1914, displayed troop parades and portraits of heads of state and diplomats. One such journal, *Review of Reviews*, carried an advertisement for reproductions of Matthew Brady's Civil War photographs. The copy for the ad claims that the American war-photographers newly arrived in France "cannot get within 100 miles of the actual fighting. . . . they rage and they fret, but they never *see* a battle" (6). The advertisement posits the Civil War as a lost Golden Age of unmediated visual perception of war, when both the photographers and civilian spectators could see "war as it really is." The American readerly and film-going public's "persistent demands for war pictures of any kind" (Mould 50) resulted in the redistribution not only of Civil War images but of any available military footage. The images of war consumed in film theaters in 1914 were not from 1914 France and Belgium but, according to newsreel industry's trade publications, "a series of old pictures showing the various armies of Europe in maneuvers [that] have been taken from the shelves" (qtd. in Mould 50). The trade publications claimed that

> Old copies of . . . kinematographic news . . . have been ransacked and often duplicated just to offer the public something that might pass for war

pictures. . . . They seem glad of pictures of mimic war if the real article cannot be obtained. . . . [T]his demand for something that looks like war is undeniably great. (qtd. in Mould 50)

A battle panorama would be one method of addressing the civilian anxiety about seeing the war from an authentic and authoritative viewing position.[4] With its promise of visual authenticity and plenitude, what the *Oxford English Dictionary* calls "an unbroken view," a panorama also both invokes and breaks with the model of vision and subjectivity found in Cartesian perspectivalism. As the dominant model of vision in Western culture since the Renaissance, perspectivalism assumes a central, privileged seeing subject. In this model, the viewer of the work of art — and of the visible world — is the unmoving, atemporal, disembodied single eye toward which the lines of perspective run.[5] I want first to emphasize the static, unmoving nature of the viewer posited by linear perspective because a panorama differs most markedly from a perspectival painting in its assumption of a mobile observer. As Crary points out, "panorama paintings clearly broke with the localized point of view of perspective painting . . . allowing the spectator an ambulatory ubiquity. One was compelled at least to turn one's head (and eyes) to see the entire work" (113).[6] Second, I want to underline the "disembodied" and "eternalized" (Jay, "Scopic Regimes" 7) quality of perspectivalism's viewer, since the panorama allows for the presence and movement of viewers' bodies in time. The panorama, in other words, gives back to the viewer the mobile physical body denied by linear perspective.

The panorama therefore could be seen as an extremely powerful model that relies on the use of a sovereign observer: central, all-seeing, and physically autonomous. And yet, the model that suggests such visual and physical autonomy for the viewer also has an overt restriction: the viewers of the largest, most popular panoramas were enclosed within buildings that housed and provided the round structure for the paintings. This conflicted model for visual experience, at once autonomous and restricted, reflects not only the model of the female observer in *Hilltop* but also reflects the contradictions that Crary finds in the construction of what he calls the "modernized" observer. Just as the panorama (both in Aldrich's text and in late nineteenth-century popular culture) provides a model of both a mobile, all-seeing observer and of a constrained or restricted seeing subject, the model of vision that began to develop in the mid-nineteenth century involved two "intertwining," apparently conflicting versions of visual experience and of the observer. Because modern optics was able to locate the source of visual experience not in the external objects of sight but rather in the tissues and nerves of the human eye, the body itself became a newly empowered, autonomous locus of vision. However, this new autonomy for the seeing eye and its body was accompanied by a growing awareness of the possibilities of erratic, idiosyncratic, and subjective vision that in turn called for new techniques of "standardization and regulation of the observer" (149–50).[7] Crary claims, "what is important is how these paths"—that of the newly autonomous and of the newly erratic and thereby regulated observer—"continually overlap in the same social terrain" (150). That overlapping or intersection of paths marks the position of the body of the female civilian observer on the militarized field of the panorama in *A Hilltop on the Marne*.

In Aldrich's text, the panorama, with its possibilities for a mobile and privileged viewer, is the central site of struggle between a civilian woman and soldiers over how to see the war,[8] and with its promise of an "unbroken view," it is a powerful metaphor for the workings of military propaganda on the civilian seeing-subject. As chapter 1 discusses, the aim of war propaganda is to construct a unified national subject; a nation at war cannot brook any difference of view. The discourses of militarism, embodied in *Hilltop* by the narratives of soldiers billeted in Aldrich's village, attempt to create an "unbroken view" of the war and a unified subject that does not differ from the Allied cause. But that same panorama also includes the possibilities for other, differing visions of the war.

At the center of the book is the scene in which Aldrich "sees" the Battle of the Marne from her garden as it invades the visual field of her panorama. Aldrich, describing her view, compares Napoleonic painting's depiction of battle with what she perceives: "I had imagined long lines of marching soldiers, detachments of flying cavalry, like the war pictures at Versailles and Fontainebleau. Now I was actually seeing a battle, and it was nothing like that. There was only noise, belching smoke, and long drifts of white clouds concealing the hill" (146).

According to Michael Marrinan, battle paintings such as those on display at Versailles and Fontainebleau and executed under Napoleon's orders were, when first exhibited, accompanied by texts "derived—either by direct quotation or close paraphrase—"from the army bulletins that Napoleon himself wrote in order to control the interpretation of the outcomes of battles (186). In her most "direct" vision of battle, what Aldrich looks at and into is a network of visual and verbal discourse about war that screens her retinal perception of battle as effectively as the smoke over the plain. Norman Bryson writes that "between the retina and world is inserted a *screen* of signs, a screen consisting of all the multiple discourses on vision built into the social arena" ("The Gaze in the Expanded Field" 92; italics in the original). The shadow of Napoleonic visual representation of battle (and the echo of Napoleonic narrative) function as the only available screen through which Aldrich (and by extension her readers) can understand her visual perception, even when this visual model is clearly inadequate and is called into question.

Despite her description of this visual screen, Aldrich writes in a letter placed immediately after the one containing her narrative of the day of the battle, "I had seen the war" (154). The primary conflict represented in this text is not the Battle of the Marne but the battle between Aldrich and the soldiers that takes place on the ground of the female gaze and its panorama, over her act of looking at the battlefield and over defining what she sees there. Two days after the battle, Aldrich is visited by French soldiers billeted in her village who want to see the view of the Marne battlefield and who ask her to "explain the country" to them. Aldrich writes of her own resistance to looking at the view:

> I had not been out there since Saturday night—was it less than 48 hours before? But . . . I was ashamed to refuse. It would, I know, seem super-sentimental to them. So I reluctantly followed them out. They stood in a group about me . . . while I pointed out the towns and answered their questions. . . .
>
> There was a young lieutenant in the group who finally noticed a sort of reluctance on my part—which I evidently had not been able to conceal—to looking off at the plain, which I own I had been surprised to find as lovely as ever. He taxed me with it, and I confessed, upon which he said:—

"That will pass. The day will come — Nature is so made, luckily — when you will look off there with pride, not pain, and be glad that you saw what may prove the turning of the tide in the noblest war ever fought for civilization."

I wonder. (156)

Aldrich's reluctance to look at the site/sight of the battlefield and the words "I wonder" mark small but resilient points of resistance to the soldier's narrative re-vision of civilian sight. Her reluctance to look, even at a plain that appears unchanged, suggests that looking at the battlefield is not an act of direct retinal perception nor of passive spectatorship but rather the conflicted act of an observer within the realm of militarizing vision. The soldiers later on in this exchange use a theater metaphor to define Aldrich's privileged viewing position: "'you can always say you had front row stage box'" (178). The workings of militaristic discourse here rely on blurring the distinction between spectator and observer: the successful mobilization of the gendered civilian subject depends on the illusion of passive spectatorship and on the veiling of the discursive techniques that construct militarized observers. I read this encounter between Aldrich and the soldiers as a parable of the watershed-moment in military visuality that the Battle of the Marne constituted. The soldiers, in re-viewing the visual field, attempt to construct the observer as a passive spectator at the "last romantic battle," a military spectacle that in fact required intense regulation of its observers.

The soldier's interpretation of the battle also marks an overlapping between image and narrative. According to the military "caption" of the view, Aldrich has seen neither smoke nor the wounding and destruction of bodies, but history itself. The soldier's words constitute a historical narrative in the future tense, a projection of the later interpretation of the Battle of the Marne. Like the panoramic battle paintings at Versailles, Aldrich's visual experience of battle is accompanied by an official military narrative. The soldier's narrative construes Aldrich as both a viewer of war and a potential reader of military history and propaganda.[9]

This slippage between seeing and reading helps further to reinforce the identification of the wartime observer as a passive civilian "spectator" of military history's plots. As in the war posters that were ubiquitous in Europe and the United States during the war, the combined codes of image and word in *Hilltop* can be read as a way for militaristic discourse to control as many sign systems as possible. Like *Fighting France*, *Hilltop* participates in a truce between word and image, but it does so through its use of photographs and a map that represent the panorama for readers. This visual apparatus in conjunction with the text functions as a way to construct Aldrich's readers as the seeing subjects of military propaganda. However, I want to trace how the visual/verbal nexus also creates possibilities for alternative or resisting wartime reading and seeing.

The panorama and its visual representations provide the text's first opportunities to induct the readerly gaze into the field of militaristic discourse. In her first contact with the British army during the first weeks of the war, a captain billeted in her village asks to be shown the view of the country from Aldrich's garden. What is exchanged here is not just information but possession of the landscape and of the way to see it. The captain points to villages within the panorama, asks Aldrich their names and their distances, studies the landscape through binoculars, looks at his map, and concludes, "I have it" (78). Opposite the text containing this dialogue is a photo of "A Part of the Panorama from the Lawn" with pencilled-in names of the visible towns. Readers can also consult the map that makes up the end papers of the book. This map is a mixture of military and civilian information, with hand-written place-names, some of which are underlined to denote visibility from Aldrich's garden, according to the handwritten legend in the lower left-hand corner. The printed legend to the right is more military in character, indicating sites of battles and troop movements. Both the photograph and the map allow Aldrich's readers to replicate as closely as possible the captain's visual experience.[10]

Along with and within the panorama, there is a second governing verbal/visual trope within this text: the index or pointing-toward that we have already seen at work in *Fighting France*. The most overt instances of indexing in the text are of course the physical gestures of both Aldrich and the soldiers, as they point toward towns within Aldrich's panorama. These gestures have several, and often contradictory, functions. Like the panorama, the act of pointing both restricts and allows for the possibility of authorial and readerly resistance to the soldiers' stories. The soldiers' acts of pointing trace the required trajectory of vision, the arc of sight that the militarized observer must follow. While the soldier pointing out villages and asking for place-names is directing and militarizing Aldrich's and her readers' vision, Aldrich is also pointing out places and "explaining the country" to the soldiers. The gesture reinforces writerly authority and authenticity (as we have already seen, a crucial issue for women writing eyewitness war narratives), because it allows the writer to emphasize physically her proximity to the scene of combat.

The map and photographs in *Hilltop* participate in the indexing, the direction and restriction, of readerly vision in several ways. First, they allow for at least a partial replication of the soldiers' vision of the landscape: as readers look at the photograph and map, the place-names are already elements in a military strategy and history, and the reader's gaze is directed along the arc of the soldier's gesture. Second, these visual elements within a primarily verbal text also act as "pointers" to guide readerly vision through their very juxtaposition with the verbal text. According to Marrinan, the visual-verbal dynamic is itself indexical, creating "a rhythm of reading, pointing, and gesturing between the text and image." A narrative accompanied by a visual image "generates a series of pointing gestures across the space anchored by the text, the image, and the reader/viewer" (187). This visual and verbal network of text, map, and photograph constructs for the reader/viewer of *Hilltop* a screen of signs similar to the Napoleonic screen through which Aldrich first sees the Battle of the Marne, constructing the reader as well as the narrator of this text as an observer of the war.

In another example of how *A Hilltop on the Marne* constructs its narrator and its readers as militarized viewers, Aldrich describes her panoramic view of the Battle of the Marne, returning to an extensive use of the place-names that also appear in the map and the photograph:

The sun was shining brilliantly on silent Mareuil and Chauconin, but Monthyon and Penchard were enveloped in smoke. . . . Owing to the smoke hanging over the crest of the hill on the horizon, it was impossible to get an idea of the positions of the armies. In the west it seemed to be somewhere near Claye, and the east it was in the direction of Barcy. I tried to remember what the English soldiers had said, — that the Germans were, if possible to be pushed east, in which case the artillery at the west must be either the French or English. The hard thing to bear was, that it was all conjecture. (146)

In order for the long list of place-names to make sense, readers would have to once again re-enact the gaze of the officer, treating the book itself like a military guidebook, referring to the photo and map. But Aldrich herself also finds her familiar landscape defamiliarized and militarized. She refers to her memory of a soldier's voice speaking of strategy in order to understand what she sees in the newly prescribed limits of her panorama. What she and her readers see — and don't see — must be "captioned" with military language; the soldier's narrative must anchor the sight to give it meaning.

However, neither the civilian reader nor author, re-enacting the soldier's gaze and re-inscribing the soldier's narrative, can possess the war's landscape and say, like the soldier learning place-names from Aldrich, "I have it." It is, as Aldrich states, all conjecture. For the female civilian observer, seeing the war constitutes a visual exile: any implicit theories of unmediated, unsocialized perception or of the sovereignty of the seeing-subject at the center of the panorama disappear. Readers and author rely first on military visual apparatus, particularly maps, and then on military narrative as a way of making meaning.

And yet, within the visual and verbal screen or net of directed militaristic vision, there are some snags, some tears in the fabric of militaristic discourse that might allow a 1915 reader of Aldrich's text to slip out of its enclosure. Although the map and photograph attempt to recreate for the reader the panorama and its illusion of a central and mobile observer, the visual-verbal interaction itself creates for the reader multiple, shifting viewpoints. Marrinan writes that in a viewing/reading situation, "The spectator, though not moving, is engaged imaginatively in several kinds of simultaneous actions in different locales" (187). The legend on the map allows for one such potential site of readerly mobility and resistance. The printed legend on the right names a town near Aldrich's home as the place "where my ambulance broke" — an episode not described in any of the letters that make up the text. Here, the verbal signs of the legend fail to "anchor" the image,[11] to guide and restrict the reader/viewer's understanding of the visual text. The visual-verbal nexus creates, in its "rhythm of reading, pointing, and gesturing," a space of readerly escape from a unified narrative, a unified visual/verbal message, and, by extension, a potential interruption in propaganda's project of creating an "unbroken view" of the Allied cause.

Aldrich's gestures of pointing reflect the contradiction discussed in chapter 1, the problem of drawing attention away from and toward the physical presence of the female civilian on the field of the panorama; the body of the female observer becomes the site of conflict in *Hilltop*. A passage from the letter written immediately after the Battle of the Marne shows that the female civilian's resisting gaze on the field of the militarized panorama must not only be anchored or captioned by the narrative line of war propaganda, or directed by gestural and textual indices, but must be controlled physically by the soldiers themselves. Another soldier looking over the landscape suddenly turns his gaze onto Aldrich herself, when he has "caught" her "looking in the other direction" away from the panorama and asks why "you — a foreigner and a woman happen to be living in what looks like exile — all alone on the top of a hill — in war time" (177). Here, the panorama and the female civilian both become the objects of the soldier's gaze. The panorama is no longer the ground of her vision and subjectivity but the background upon which she becomes the gendered and nationalized object of the military male gaze. She becomes, in other words, a visual element of the battle panorama that now revolves around the soldier as central seeing subject, recalling the way the battle panoramas that Napoleon had constructed in Paris included live trees and actors in the middle distance between the central viewing platform and canvas (Lawson 89). Aldrich answers the soldier's question in terms of vision, attempting to reassert her slipping subject position as the central viewer of the landscape, and one who denounces the war's violence in visual terms:

> I had chosen this hilltop for the sake of the panorama spread out before me; . . . I had loved it every day more than the day before; and . . . exactly three months after I had sat down on the hill top this awful war had marched to within sight of my gate, and banged its cannon and flung its deadly bombs right under my eyes. (178)

This civilian's narrative of the Battle of the Marne creates another conflict in the text, this time a physical one: "Do you know, every mother's son of them threw back his head—and laughed aloud. I was startled. I knew that I had shown unnecessary feeling—but I knew it too late. I made a dash for the house, but the lieutenant blocked the way. I could not make a scene. I never felt so like it in my life" (178).

Aldrich is physically denied the mobility that the panorama promises the observer (a promise that is bound to be broken), and in being so blocked from escaping the site/sight of the battlefield, she is also prohibited from "making a scene." The binary subject-object model of vision here seems to grow uncertain: to make a scene, to introduce the resisting look of an imperfectly militarized seeing subject, is also to run the risk of becoming an object in the landscape under the soldier's gaze—of making a spectacle of herself. Mary Russo describes the combination of will and loss-of-control that characterizes the woman-as-spectacle within a patriarchal specular economy, observing that "making a spectacle out of oneself seem[s] a specifically feminine danger. The danger [is] of exposure.... For a woman, making a spectacle out of herself [has] . . . to do with a kind of inadvertency and loss of boundaries" (213).

By complying with the soldiers' physically enforced gaze, Aldrich resubmits her own gaze to militaristic boundaries, to the highly regulated model of the seeing subject required for a militarized observer. This process reflects Mary Anne Doane's claim that "when the woman looks in order to see, the trajectory of that gaze, and its relation to the . . . opposition between subject and object, are highly regulated" (177). That trajectory is, as Aldrich's text suggests, even more highly regulated in wartime.

Aldrich's panorama constitutes one corner of the contradictory, gendered terrain of modernized vision during World War I, where the female civilian body at the shifting center of the war's landscape is both the subject and object of militarized vision and the source of resistance to it. Through its letters to an unnamed correspondent, the narrative structure of *Hilltop* reflects not the centralized seeing subject of panoramas, but rather a dialogic subject, constituted by the textual gestures of pointing back and forth across the space of correspondence. The letter form itself creates "a rhythm of reading, pointing, and gesturing" (Marrinan 187), a screen of signs across textual space, but it is a screen marked by gaps—

gaps around the space of the correspondent, the unrecorded responses of Gertrude Stein and Alice B. Toklas. Mary Jacobus suggests that the textual model of letters between women provides an interplay of identity and difference between correspondents. Jacobus claims that while letters initiate a correspondence or resemblance between readers, "the textual interchange of dialogue refuses the specular structure of frozen resemblance," thus creating "a play of difference or a liberating exchange" (281). Stein herself, in the manuscript "Mildred Aldrich Saturday," quoted in this chapter's epigraph, associates Aldrich's wartime vision with visual difference: "not exactly the same as any one can see war and more not exactly the same as anyone can see." Aldrich's visual difference, the remainder or excess of visual resistance on the unifying panoramic field, runs counter to the kind of specularizing nationalism that Stein identifies in "Patriarchal Poetry": "Patriarchal poetry is the same as Patriotic poetry is the same as patriarchal poetry is the same as Patriotic poetry is the same as patriarchal poetry is the same" (115).[12] If, as Jacobus reminds us, "without difference there is nothing but freezing identity" and "*in*difference" (280), Aldrich's letters to the unnamed Stein and Toklas initiate a gesture that can attempt to fracture with difference militarism's unbroken view.

2

Regarding Fascism

3

A *Stricken Field* and the Field of Vision: Fascism, Gender, and the Specular

ARTHA GELLHORN'S 1940 NOVEL *A STRICKEN FIELD*, set in Prague, in October 1938, immediately following the Nazi invasion of Czechoslovakia, provides a range of gendered seeing positions within, and in opposition to, the visual ideologies of fascism for both its characters and its readers. I am interested in examining how *A Stricken Field* works as an antifascist text, not only in its content or "subject matter" (Nazi terrorizing, torture, and murder of Czech citizens and German Communist refugees) but also in its very construction of vision: in its inscriptions of what is visible and what is invisible and how it reveals and conceals events from its characters' and its readers' sight.

The novel explores the importance as well as the failures or limits of women's vision under Nazism primarily through the gazes of its two female protagonists, an American journalist named Mary Douglas and a German Communist refugee, Rita. My suggestion is that in this text it is representations of vision and loss of vision that re-create for the novel's readers the brutal assault on subjectivity (both individual and collective) perpetrated by fascism and that attempt to construct readers as potentially antifascist readers/observers.[1] A *Stricken Field* demonstrates how vision — and, by extension, the seeing subject — is exposed to control, torture, and loss under a fascist regime. It also suggests that a differently constructed vision is essential for readerly resistance to and understanding of the effects of the Third Reich's invasion policy and its aesthetic and sexual ideologies. I am concerned with how this novel constructs that difference through the female gaze and the failures of that gaze in order to offer its readers possible alternatives to what Linda Mizejewski calls "the Nazi cult of the visual" (4). Within the complexities and contradictions of that gaze, political seeing is closely connected to problems of female sexuality and to what becomes the text's always deferred visual referent: the torture of Czech Communists working against the Third Reich.

Scholars such as Russell Berman and Thomas Elsaesser have begun to explore the position of visual discourses in fascist ideology. Berman outlines what he calls "a fascist privileging of sight and visual representation" and claims that "fascist modernist" works such as *Triumph of the Will* define and enact "a fascist rhetoric as the displacement of verbal by visual representation" (100). If Berman is right, several questions arise for me in reading Gellhorn's novel *A Stricken Field*: Is the "privileging of sight and visual representation" always somehow "fascist"? (How) is sight — particularly women's sight — to be recuperated in an antifascist text?

I find helpful here Elsaesser's characterization of fascism as "the specularization of social, sexual, and political life" (548); for Elsaesser, it is specularization, rather than a more general "privileging sight and visual representation," that best characterizes fascist visuality. Fascism, with what Mizejewski characterizes as its "obsession with both difference and sameness" (32), can, as Elsaesser suggests, be in part understood as a grotesque extreme of specular thought. The subject of Nazi ideology, like the subject of specular thinking, wants to see the Same, and fascism used every available technology (from visual art to weapons of mass destruction) to further its project of eradicating difference within the Third Reich.[2] I read the project of *A Stricken Field* as the attempt to inscribe a politicized, antifascist female gaze (within the text, in its characters) that refuses specularization, and thereby to construct its American readers as anti-fascist observers.

I would like first to look at passages of *A Stricken Field* that outline possible positions for the American observer through the point of view of Mary Douglas. I will then examine how the narrative moves past the limitations of what Mary can see to how the reader might be constructed through Rita's point of view: that is, through Rita's vision and loss of vision. In using the phrase "point of view," I want to emphasize "view," the gazes of these characters represented in the text, and how these gazes construct the novel's characters and readers as observers of fascist politics.

One of the novel's central issues explored by the juxtaposition of Mary's and Rita's sight is the ideal and limitations of "complete" and "direct" vision during wartime. This issue is raised immediately in the novel's epigraph, a passage identified only as being "from a Medieval Chronicle," that locates the text squarely in the territory where military violence, vision, and gender intersect:

> There were young knights among them who had never been present at a stricken field. Some could not look upon it and some could not speak and they held themselves apart from the others who were cutting down the prisoners at my Lord's orders, for the prisoners were a body too numerous to be guarded by those of us who were left. Then . . . an aged knight . . . who had been sore wounded in the battle, rode up to the group of young knights and said, "Are ye maidens with your downcast eyes? Look well upon it. See all of it. Close your eyes to nothing. For a battle is fought to be won. And it is this that happens if you lose." (1)

The narrator's shifting pronouns, from third to first and back to third person make the subject and object of the enunciation difficult to identify. Who is the speaker of the passage? To whom is this emphatic, repeated injunction to see everything addressed? How is it to be understood as a metaphor for the work of the novel as a whole? The slippage between third and first person narrative ("young knights," "those of us who were left") suggests that this call might be addressed to any combination of the novel's characters, author, and/or readers. This slippage itself would seem to both enact and undercut the completeness of vision for which the knight calls:

the pronouns both include a range of possible subject-positions and disperse and fragment those positions.[3]

As a call to vision and against a maidenly aversion to seeing, the epigraph asserts the possibility and importance of direct perception of the effects of war. This is what the novel itself radically questions: the power of an all-encompassing and direct vision, one associated with masculinity, under fascism. Paul Virilio claims that after the widespread use of reconnaissance planes using optical technologies in World War I, "*Direct vision was now a thing of the past*" (11). Seeing "all of it" (like the promise of Aldrich's panorama with its "unbroken view") is the undercut ideal for antifascist observers — and, as I hope to show, is indirectly associated with fascist visuality. It is instead the "downcast eyes" associated with "maidens" that takes the place of this ideal of complete vision for Gellhorn's characters and readers.[4] This casting down of the ideal of complete, direct vision, embodied in the several models of the female gaze at and under Nazi political power, is also a route by which the text attempts an escape from or alternative to fascist visuality.

Immediately following the epigraph's call for complete vision, the novel's first chapter opens with a questioning of "the reliability of the image" (Mizejewski 19), as Mary Douglas and her fellow passengers fly over Europe on their way to Prague:

> From this height the Rhine looked narrow, sluggish, and unimportant. When they were over Germany everyone leaned close to the windows, staring out as if they hoped to see something special. But the land looked the same as when they flew across France, summer green and rich. . . . Perhaps the roofs are steeper, she thought, but the land doesn't look any different. . . . Later someone said, "this is occupied territory," and again they pressed at the windows, expecting some change in the land to equal the change on the map. There was nothing to see. What are we looking for, she wondered, maybe a swastika painted on a roof? (3)

While for Wharton an imagined aerial view held out at least the promise of an escape from the disorienting vision of trench warfare, here, the disorientation brought about by Nazi Germany's military conquests is only exacerbated by an actual aerial perspective. Like Wharton straining her eyes obediently for evidence of the enemy in *Fighting France*, the group on the airplane is looking for signs of the enemy's visible difference. This disjunction between retinal perception of a landscape and how that landscape is represented on maps establishes the novel's first instance of the immense limitations of vision under fascism, the impossibility of a comprehensive vision, even as vision is asserted as a primary tool of understanding political change and oppression.

This same kind of absence of signs and the failure or refusal of vision to account for or make sense of Nazi-enforced political boundaries is described in the middle of the novel, when Mary drives to the newly drawn Czech-German frontier. In this scene, however, the confrontation between fascist signs and resisting vision becomes more pronounced, as the American observer encounters a gradually accumulating set of signs of the new political order. At first, Mary again encounters a frontier that is remarkable for its very invisibility:

> There was nothing wrong with the road, there was no sign up, there was nothing to tell you: but the road was condemned. The country had come to an end. . . . "That is Germany now," . . . [the chauffeur] said, and pointed ahead.
> "I don't understand."
> He looked at her. "Nobody does. But if we drive on, after a while we will meet the German soldiers."
> "But isn't there a frontier post or something, how do know where you are?"
> "Sometimes there is. Not here." (111)

Mary's first encounter with some visible sign of the frontier is with a group of Czech civilians whose very act of looking at the frontier itself constitutes a confusing and alarming spectacle, as if the act of looking itself helped to constitute the frontier: "Then up ahead, they saw a group of people standing in the road. 'What are they doing?' Mary asked. 'What is happening here?' 'They are looking,' the chauffeur said" (111–12).

The next piece of visible evidence that Mary sees underlines the arbitrary nature of political signs under the Nazi regime:

> No one talked. They stood in the road and stared at a piece of barbed wire that was pegged into the ground over the road and cut short on either side.
> "That's the frontier," the chauffeur explained.

> She looked at it with absolute unbelief. You do not simply peg up fifty feet of barbed wire and proclaim a new rule. You did not drive people from their homes or jail them or shoot them, confiscate property and deny their language and the old forms of life, and then lay down fifty feet of barbed wire to prove it. (112)

This act of looking, as it seems to actually reinforce the border, also creates a temporary collective of resisting vision of which Mary is a part. This collective vision of the Czech citizens participates in the text's larger project of inscribing the Czech victims of the invasion as subjects as well as objects of politicized sight:

> The people beside her were looking at the barbed wire with the same shocked, unbelieving faces. Why here? Why not farther ahead or farther behind? The land on the other side belonged to the land on this side; it had the same shape. . . . Oh, no, she told herself, I don't believe it. Why don't we lift the pegs ourselves and move the silly frontier . . . ?
> Then she saw the soldier. (112)

The resisting vision that refuses to see the difference in the landscape focuses not only on the arbitrariness but also on the paucity of the sign of the Nazis' political power. The barbed wire as a metonym for the invasion must be reinforced by the German soldier, who functions as another, more complex sign, one capable of signifying not only Nazi power but also the physical reinforcement of that power:

> The Czechs watched him, not saying anything, not moving, their faces blank and polite. The boy . . . tried to stare the Czechs down. . . . Mary Douglas stared at him, fascinated like the others, unbelieving. But he was true, he stood six feet in his field-gray uniform, with his square steel helmet and heavy boots and his rifle; he was part of the army that had overrun the land, and behind him lay Czechoslovakia . . . but now it was called Germany and he was on guard. . . . And she thought . . . the land is exactly the same, on the other side of the barbed wire. (112–14)

The German soldier is identified first through metonymy and then synecdoche: he is identified with his equipment, the elements of his uniform (helmet, boots, rifle) and then with the army of which he is part. The soldier also represents another position on the map of political gazes that this text traces: the policing, threatening gaze of the Nazi regime (a gaze that grows more important to the narrative as the text progresses and to which I will return at the end of the chapter).

What the characters and readers of this scene are witnessing are the first visible signs of the Third Reich's political power, inscribed on the landscape before their eyes. Mary's and the readers' gaze moves from the utter absence of signs to the material sign of the barbed wire, then to the soldier: increasingly complex (and physically threatening) tropes for political borders and for the ability to reinforce those borders. This buildup of increasingly complex signs on/as the frontier might be understood in the context of Jeffrey Schnapp's claim that "fascism required an aesthetic *overproduction*, a surfeit of fascist signs, images, slogans, books, and buildings, in order to compensate for, fill in, and cover up its forever unstable ideological core" (3). The witnesses in the scene at the frontier are seeing not only signs of the fascist frontier but also the very *frontier of fascist signs*, the earliest stages of such sign (over)production, as if they were a theater audience watching not a play but its stage-set in the process of being built. However, I want to emphasize that these observers at the frontier of fascist signs are not passive spectators but, to use again Crary's terms, intensely regulated observers. The characters looking at the newly inscribed frontier are being inducted into a visuality that condenses the Nazi's power in Czechoslovakia to its simplest material signs: a piece of barbed wire, a helmet, a rifle. These are then perceived as part of an increasingly complex network of signs. *A Stricken Field* attempts in this scene to replicate for its American readers both the Third Reich's regulation of vision and the observer's act of resistance: the look that refuses to acknowledge the strict difference of land on either side of the new frontier.

In considering how the novel works as an antifascist text, I suggest that these visions of sameness, of the lack of visible difference between Nazi-occupied and "free" territory, are in fact not so much "failures" of "complete" vision as they are one way for *A Stricken Field* to counter an important element of Nazi ideology: the insistence on the imposition of strict boundaries, of visible, irreconcilable difference as a means of identifying, isolating, excoriating, and ultimately destroying the Other. Under the

Third Reich, that Other was identified in terms of political ideology, race, ethnicity, and gender. Linda Mizejewski writes that "[i]n the biological order that the Third Reich worked to attain, the visible differences of gender and race served to confirm a 'natural' hierarchy" (14). The absolute line between Germany and Czechoslovakia can be read as a geographic metaphor of the strict binary differences of race and gender that fascism sought to maintain in its specular search for "racial purity." Mizejewski claims that it is the questioning of the reliability of the visible, particularly in the realm of ethnic difference, that acts to destabilize fascist boundaries of identity: "The complication and frustration of the Reich's aim for visible, natural difference recurs in its aim for ethnic purity. Jewishness, unlike sex and race, is 'invisible,' and thus tests German fascism's privileging of visibility, the reliability of the image" (18).

In her foreword to Klaus Theweleit's *Male Fantasies*, Barbara Ehrenreich claims that leftist politics and female sexuality also presented a perceived threat to the stability of fascist signs: the breakdown of barriers "is what the fascist held himself in horror of, and what he saw in communism, in female sexuality" (xvii).

As an antifascist work, *A Stricken Field* precipitates a crisis over "the reliability of the image," writing the "failure" of seeing as a way to avoid its co-optation by a fascist visuality that requires its subjects to see inherent and permanent difference. The airplane and frontier scenes of the failure of "complete" vision (and the possibility that "failure" is a mode of resistance) prefigure later failures or blocks in the text's visual representations of both female sexuality and the Gestapo torture of political prisoners.

A Stricken Field removes crucial events—specifically, the sight of Nazi atrocities and torture—from the characters' and readers' fields of vision, writing into the text heavily marked gaps in vision or instances of "downcast eyes." In a dialogue in chapter 2 between Mary and her fellow journalists (all of whom are men, and almost all are American), there are several references to the witnessing of physical atrocities perpetrated by the Nazi regime, references marked by a conflict in or absence of visual representation. If the scene at the Czech-German frontier inscribes the gradual accumulation of signs of Nazi political power, this long dialogue among the journalists performs a different but equally important function, as if it were drawing an ever smaller series of concentric circles around the witnessing of the most brutal of Gestapo acts, but finally always defers any visual representation of political atrocities. One of the American journalists, describing his rescuing of his Czech chauffeur from a Nazi prison, says, "'I've seen people scared. . . . But this boy was scared of something you couldn't see'" (22). This underscoring of the absence of visual representation of Nazi atrocity, its invisibility to Western eyes, is intensified when another of Mary's colleagues tells her, "'if you hang around the frontier . . . and go to the places the refugees are staying, . . . you will see things that will alarm and surprise you. In the way of messiness, I mean. You will also hear things that are worse, but you can't check them, so you have to throw them out'" (23). The unspecified, invisible presence of the things "you will see . . . that will alarm and disturb you" accumulates still further in this passage:

> "The only one who has seen a first-class atrocity," Tompkins said, "is Markton . . . from the *Daily Clarion*. My paper wouldn't use it, but his gives him a bonus. And he's an honest lad; he wouldn't make it up, the way most of their men would. He really did see it."
>
> None of them asked to hear the story. . . . the others were shying away from it, as if they had heard too much, and seen too much. (23–24)

Again, the absence of what the journalist has seen leaves a heavily marked gap in the text, both an insistence on and a removal of visual perception from the narrative. Like the emphatically gestured toward and always deferred vision of war in *Fighting France*, acts of torture are indexed more and more in this novel, and this increased verbal pointing serves to underscore the *in*visibility of Nazi atrocities in the narrative.

As the journalists' dialogue circles closer to a representation of the full force of Nazi brutality, the construction of the journalistic gaze also suggests that acts of seeing atrocities are construed as commodities, acts that simultaneously privilege the visual experiences of journalists of "free" countries and devalue what the Czech and German victims of the Third Reich see. This becomes especially clear when Thane, another of the journalists, tells to the group a brief biography of Rita. His narrative includes the Gestapo's torture and murder of her brother in Germany several years before the events represented in the novel:

> "They slapped her face so she'd keep her eyes open and watch it, and they kept it up with the belt buckle until they'd laid his kidneys bare and after a while he died."
>
> "Right there?" the novelist said in a quiet voice. "Right there in front of her?"
>
> "Right there in front of her." . . .
>
> "Some story," Tompkins said. "I wonder if I could use it anyway?"
>
> "There must be about five thousand others, as a minimum, just like it in Prague alone," Thane said. (28–29)

This passage establishes Rita's identity in the act of witnessing torture and in the transformation of that witnessing not only into a narrative that might or might not be "used" but that is representative of thousands of similar stories—and therefore "unusable." Her status as a seeing-subject is, in other words, understood in so far as it is subject to control and torture by the fascist regime and as it is representative of a collective, "unusable" narrative of the fascist control of vision, devalued in the economy of journalistic narrative.

The journalist's devaluing of Rita's status as a witness, as a seeing-subject because of her political identity as a refugee and a Communist is also intimately connected to gender and sexuality, to Rita as the object of a male political and sexual gaze: "'What does she look like?' Tom Lambert said. 'Like nothing,' Thane said. 'Like a she-communist'" (29). Thane's characterization of what Rita "looks like" attempts both to render her invisible (she looks like nothing) and, in calling her a "she-communist," to identify her as a part of a political collective in a way that both genders and dehumanizes, as if "communist" were some form of animal life. Another implication of Thane's statement is that while he emphasizes Rita's gender, he de-emphasizes her sexuality: to "look like nothing" could easily translate as "to fit no requisite standards of female beauty and, by extension, sexual value." However, Thane's description of Rita as looking "like nothing" also suggests the threatening invisibility of female sexuality, the "nothing-to-be-seen" that marks sexual difference in psychoanalytic theory. In Thane's description, the "nothing" that constitutes Rita as the object of his gaze is a gendered, politicized, and sexualized nothing.

This gendering and politicizing male gaze is paralleled and countered by Mary's silent response to the question of what Rita looks like, as she attempts to recuperate Rita as an object of a sexualizing *female* gaze. Mary remembers two encounters with Rita: the first had taken place before the Nazi invasion, just after Rita's release from a German prison and her immigration to Prague; the second has taken place earlier in the evening, an encounter described in the novel's first chapter and to which I will return in more detail later in the chapter. Mary's memory of the two encounters is as follows:

> In May, Mary thought, Rita didn't really have a face: just eyes, a mouth, a nose. . . . But she was wonderful to look at anyway, or why did we all keep turning towards her corner, when she never said a word. She had something none of us had, certainly. This evening . . . when she said, "Now I go home," she wasn't pretty. Only you wished you could look like that yourself; you knew with envy how the way she looked would enter in to the man waiting for her; you wanted to . . . touch her and take for yourself what she had behind her skin, behind her eyes. . . . Mary thought, with scorn, a man who knew anything about women would know what she looks like. (30)

The last few lines offer a shifting series of different locations for sexual desire and identification through vision: Mary remembers her own and "our" looking at Rita, imagines herself in the position of a man looking at Rita, and wants to look like, and be looked at like, Rita. In each of these looks, Rita is an object of a female gaze that constitutes "knowledge" about women that Mary's male colleague does not (but should) possess. What do these shifting gazes have to do with the Rita described only a few lines earlier as the forced witness of her own brother's death, as a witness subject to the most dehumanizing and terrifying control of her own vision? How do all these looks (the enforced gaze on/as torture, the gendering and politicizing look of the male journalist, Mary's shifting series of sexualizing gazes) establish parameters of sexual and political vision in response to fascism?

Mediating the extremes of the political and sexual gazes that are set in motion in the above passage is, as if in answer to the male journalist's "nothing," "something": whatever it is that made "us" (American observers) look at her. "Something" marks the visual territory where the political and sexual overlap. It marks as well the difference between what the American observer can see and what she can't, which is the very territory where so much of the narrative exists. Fiction, as opposed to reportage, is what allows Gellhorn to even begin to map out this border territory between political and sexual, between visible and invisible, between the American witness's visual subjectivity and that of a German Communist.

In order to try and define further the "something" that connects all the looks that circulate around Rita and Rita's own gaze, one might benefit from at least a rough map of the iconography of female Communists in the fascist imagination; an important source for this is Klaus Theweleit's *Male Fantasies*. Part of Theweleit's work documents the place occupied by the "Red woman" (xiv) in the writings of members of the Freikorps, the World War I military elite, many of whom went on to fight revolutionary Communists in Germany in the interwar years and eventually to enter the upper echelon of the Nazi party. The female Communist is the "Rifle-woman," the "proletarian whore" of the Red Army who represents to the "soldier males" a chain of threatening signifiers that circle around female sexuality and the dangerous politics with which it is associated: the conflated threats of uncontrolled sexuality, filth, the loss of boundaries, violence, castration, and communism (70–79). Theweleit traces one chain of sexual and political associations found in writings by Freikorps members: "*Erotic male-female relationship — violent, unfeeling woman — threat to the man — dirt, vulgarity — prostitution — proletarian woman — communism*" (70). Theweleit claims that for the early fascist soldiers the "Red woman" is "a natural catastrophe, a freak. The sexuality of the proletarian woman/gun slinging whore/communist is out to castrate and shred men to pieces" (76).

In addition to these fantasies of the "Red woman," there is another problem concerning representations of female sexuality in relation to fascism in this period. Mizejewski's analysis examines how in both prewar and postwar U.S. and British fiction, film, and theater, the rise of German fascism was troped not only in terms of Nazi spectacle but the spectacle of the Weimar Berlin "show girl," the "Sally Bowles" figure first found in

Christopher Isherwood's 1939 story of that name. Mizejewski writes that beginning with Isherwood's Sally and continuing through later American and British postwar representations, "[v]isibility is situated as a crisis that is both sexual and political, in that the hidden nature of female sexuality is conflated with the hidden sexual secret of Nazi Germany" (17–18).

It is the conflation of female sexual spectacle and political threat — whether from the left or the right — that A *Stricken Field* works to resist. The American male observer's ambivalent look at the "she-communist" who "looks like nothing" denies her sexuality even as it insists upon a sexuality that is both dehumanized and potentially politically threatening. As an antifascist text, then, the novel counters not only the fascist's terror of the "Red woman" but also an American (male) reader's potential suspicion of the threatening politics "hidden" in female sexuality. It does so partly in it attempts to represent Rita's sexuality without specularization, a project that requires significant gaps or breaks in vision and visual description in the narrative.

The problem of what Rita looks like leads to one of the most difficult projects of this novel: to represent the European victims of Nazi rule, particularly Rita, not only as objects of a sympathetic American observer's sight but *subjects* of sight. This project is an extremely conflicted one, given the restraints, torture, and loss to which Rita's vision is subject. I want to invoke deLauretis's claim that at stake in feminist criticism is "not so much how 'to make visible the invisible' as how to produce the conditions of visibility for a different social subject" (8). Gellhorn's novel, in its attempt to inscribe Rita as object and subject of sight, sets in motion both aspects of this project — and ultimately demonstrates its limits within the visuality imposed by Nazi rule. These conditions of visibility are, as it were, in the dark, most effectively produced through a blocking of vision, through blindness, darkness, and not-seeing.[5]

In the text's very first encounter with Rita, even before readers or Mary are aware of her having witnessed her brother's death, she is understood in terms of vision. Mary's first-chapter meeting with Rita on a Prague street establishes important associations between vision, sexuality, and politics. Having last seen Rita five months earlier, just after Rita's release from a German prison, Mary now "saw what could be seen at once," Rita's new clothes and well-cut hair, and she thinks, "but what has changed her, she looks so well" (15). A brief narrative shift to Rita's point of view suggests not only that she is pleased at being so looked at but also that this pleasure is indirectly associated with political freedom:

> A week ago she had bought a lipstick no larger than a capsule for five pennies, and at last she had dared smear some of it on her mouth. It was the wrong color but she did not know, and only saw herself as brilliant and gay, with a face she need not hide. She saved the lipstick now, not wanting to squander it, or use it for every day. She wished that she had worn some this evening for Mary to see. (15)

These lines do not allow Rita's point of view complete narrative control; the third-person narrator intrudes on Rita's point of view ("It was the wrong color but she did not know") as if Rita were a child playing at being a grown-up woman. There are several possible effects of this narrative intrusion, depending on the political character of the novel's readers: one is to make Rita's character unthreatening to American readers fearful of Communist politics; another is to critique how other readers might underestimate Rita's abilities or view her politics as naive, much as Thane does in his narrative of Rita and her brother: "'Of course they were crazy, the way honest Communists are, you know, believing in it like the second coming of Christ. . . . They were just little intellectuals who worked for a better world'" (27). Both attitudes toward Rita are overturned later in the novel as the text eventually requires the reader to trust Rita and her visual experience. Another possible effect of the narrative intrusion is to see Rita's unfamiliarity with lipstick and her self-conscious use of it as an emphasis on miming, on the act of display, on making visible the performance of the signs of female sexuality and associating it with political freedom — "a face she need not hide."

The connection between Rita's willingness to be seen and the dangers of her political position are underscored when Mary remembers her very first meeting with Rita five months earlier, just after Rita's release from prison, a memory that acknowledges the dangers of visibility to a refugee: "Rita seemed to fear that sooner or later they [American journalists in Prague] would use what they knew of her, and identify her . . . and she kept distrust of everyone. All she wanted then, Mary had guessed, was to disappear, . . . not to be noticed ever again, not to be caught" (17).

The connection between how Rita looks now, her willingness to be seen, her politics, and her sexuality is further elaborated in this scene in Mary's reflection on Rita's statement, "Now I go home": "She said 'home' shyly . . . , as if it were a rare word, and one that she wanted Mary to hear. If it weren't so idiotic, Mary told herself, I'd begin to imagine that she has a fine house, a fine husband, four fine children and at least a British passport" (17).

The series of impossible positions that Mary imagines for Rita—a wife, a mother, a property owner, a citizen of a country outside of the Third Reich—suggests how gender and governmental politics are intimately connected. Rita, as a refugee and a Communist, is denied the status of wife and mother that would constitute her as a woman in the Third Reich.[6] The narrative requires that the readers accept Rita as a woman without the socially recognized signs of female citizenship within patriarchy.

The chapter closes with further connection between Rita's visibility, her "home" life, her sexuality, and her political status when Mary thinks, "Rita's not a refugee anymore. It's finished. She's lost that floating, empty-hearted look they have. She's happy. That's the same thing as having a country, anyhow" (18).

This encounter between Mary and Rita, with its crossing of their points of view, establishes a chain of political, sexual, and visual meanings that I would juxtapose with—and view as a possible answer to—the one Theweleit uses in *Male Fantasies* to track the signification of the "Red woman." This chain of significance would link performance of "female-ness," sexual and political visibility, having a home, and democracy. If Rita's status as a refugee separates her from the signs of "safe" (both in fascist and nonfascist culture) womanhood (marriage, motherhood, home), the text attempts to reinscribe Rita's sexuality and indirectly relate it to democracy. Part of the novel's work as an antifascist text is its insistence on rendering Rita's sexuality unthreatening for an American readership, associating it with political freedom—in other words, making a Red woman's sexuality safe for democracy.

As I have suggested earlier, the ultimate and always deferred visual referent for the female observers (and by extension, the readers) of this text is the unseen fact of torture. Two crucial events of the narrative, events that frame Rita's presence in the text, are scenes of death-by-torture by Nazi agents. The first, as we have seen, is the death-by-torture of Rita's brother, an event that has already occurred at the time of narration. The second, occurring near the end of the novel, is the death of Rita's lover, Peter, another German Communist refugee working on an underground party paper in Prague. However, the visual experience that is central to Rita's character and to the narrative is outside the narrative's and readers' direct line of vision. Along with Thane's narrative, there are several other references to her witnessing of her brother's death, each of them narrated from Rita's point of view and each, like the English journalist's sight of atrocity, kept invisible.

In the middle of the novel, Rita recounts to Peter a dream that underlines the mortal dangers of vision, of being both a subject and object of sight, under fascism. It also demonstrates the text's capacity for both representing and leaving inaccessible Rita's visual experience:

> "I was running through the streets—first it was Prague—everybody turned and stared at me but if they stared at me that showed the others who I was and I begged them as I ran not to look at me—please don't look at me—then it was Berlin and I went into a bakery at the corner of my father's street and begged them to hide me but they said no, no, and waved their arms and were afraid and said go away from here. . . . then I ran and all the doors closed in my face—then I ran down a long corridor and I never saw what was behind me and I came into the room."
>
> The room: the dreams always ended here.
>
> "They were standing there in their uniforms and smiling and smiling and there was a big light in the ceiling and they looked at me and laughed and then I saw what was behind them."
>
> "No," he said. "Do not speak of it, Rita." (96)

For a victim of the Gestapo, danger is troped in terms of vision. To be open to the looks of people is to be exposed to mortal, unspecified danger and to the utter control of what is seen. And again, Rita's visual experience is outside the narrative's line of sight; what she sees is not (cannot be?) contained by the text. The dream is a parable of how fascism attempts to invade and control the entire visual field (and by extension, subjectivity), as it traces Rita's movement through object and subject positions in her flight back toward the heart of fascist visuality and brutality, a primal scene left glaringly absent from the narrative. The dream suggests the political necessity of the text's "downcast eyes," of refusing to expose the potential victim of fascism to the dangers of a look that specularizes and destroys. The dream also suggests that perhaps the only subject who can — or would want to — "see all of it" or be open to being looked at by the eyes in Rita's dream is the subject of a fascist visual agenda, a subject and object of voracious political surveillance. Concerning the German majority during the Nazi era, Elsaesser writes,

> Might not the pleasure of fascism, its fascination, have been less the sadism and brutality of S.S. officers than the pleasure of being seen, of placing oneself in view of the all-seeing eye of the State? Fascism in its Imaginary encouraged a moral exhibitionism, as it encouraged denunciation and mutual surveillance. (545)

In complying with Peter's request not to speak of it, Rita keeps her final vision out of the text — another way in which the novel offers a "failure" of sight as a response to fascist visuality.

In yet another passage in the middle of the novel, the text again traces the effects of being both a subject and object of vision under fascism and absents Rita's visual experience of torture when Rita thinks:

> The ones who die violently always look tired, she thought. She had seen a woman in her prison who died after being too long in the basement cells; she had not been beaten, but perhaps what went on in her brain before she died was the violence. She had seen her brother on the floor under the bright light. She had seen . . . (153; ellipses in the original)

This memory, like the dream, creates another gap around the sight of torture, another space held open for the reader to imagine — and finally to trust — Rita's sight. For the novel's readers, it is literally blind trust of what Rita has seen that is crucial to the readers' own participation in the antifascist work of the novel. The long and profoundly disturbing penultimate chapter that includes Peter's death is narrated from Rita's point of view and describes her arriving, through information gotten from her fellow party members, at a Prague house where Peter is being held by Nazi police. Rita manages to get into the basement of the house in a series of exhausting and traumatic moves (climbing over fences, crawling through tiny passages, sliding down a coal chute) that takes ten pages to narrate. In the dark, she hears through a furnace pipe the interrogation and torture enacted in the room above. The representation of an almost complete absence of vision is crucial to the chapter. Rita's completely auditory experience of Peter's death is an act against his disappearance, even as Peter's removal from the text's (i.e., Rita's and the reader's) sight underlines that disappearance.

What Rita hears in this chapter are the voices of Gestapo officers in-terrogating Peter, the sounds of weapons being used on him, and Peter's nonverbal sounds of physical pain. The text occasionally refers directly to Rita's visual imagination ("She had seen it all; she knew how the room looked" [268]) or her refusal to imagine ("She would not think how that face looked" [265]), asking the reader to trust a visual experience not ac-cessible to the narrative. But the text accomplishes this request most effec-tively through the almost complete absence of visual description and a re-liance instead on hearing in the part of the chapter that narrates Peter's death.

Removing these scenes of torture from the text's direct line of sight has several possible and contradictory effects on its American readers, and I will be referring here to Elaine Scarry's powerful analysis of the structure of torture in *The Body in Pain* to help delineate those effects.

On the one hand, by refusing to make the reader "look" at the scene of Peter's death, the text refuses to replicate (and thereby lodges a textual protest against) the totalitarian control and torture of vision. According to Scarry, the display of a weapon, making it a focused and forced object of sight, is central to the structure of torture: "What assists the conversion of absolute pain into the fiction of absolute power is an obsessive, self-conscious display of agency. On the simplest level, the agent displayed is the weapon" (27).

By screening the scene of torture from readerly view, the text refuses to participate in or mimic torture's display. At the same time, however, the text replicates, enacts, or implements for the reader the loss of control of vision that is the fate of the victims of Nazism. *A Stricken Field*'s readers best learn the experience of Nazism's victims through the *loss* of vision. If, as the dialogue between journalists suggests, the sight of atrocity (rendered in visually descriptive language) is only a journalistic commodity, loss of vision becomes the best way for American readers to "see" the effects of Nazism.

Following her claim about the display of agency in torture, Scarry writes:

> whatever the regime's primary weapon, it is only one of many weapons and its display is only one of many endlessly multiplied acts of display: torture is a process which not only converts but announces the conversion of every available aspect of the event and the environment into an agent of pain. . . . torture is a grotesque piece of compensatory drama. (27–28)

For whom is the "grotesque compensatory drama" of torture performed? Who is its audience? Scarry notes that the language used by many regimes has emphasized the "theatrical" nature of torture (for example, referring to the room in which torture takes place as the "production room," the "cinema room," the "blue lit stage" [28]) but leaves open this question of torture's audience. The grotesque drama that is torture is a closed or closet drama, consisting only of actors (those who torture) and those who are acted upon (the prisoner). A person, such as represented by Rita, forced to witness the act of torture seems to me to be less an audience (which suggests the passivity of Crary's spectator) than another victim of torture. It is narrative representations that can open the scene of torture to an audience — or, as in the case of *A Stricken Field*, open it only partly, through hearing rather than sight. The audience in the novel's scene of torture (Rita and the readers) are auditors rather than spectators, and it is through such hearing that the readers and characters are constructed as resisting observers of the fascist regime in Czechoslovakia. In the harrowing reading experience of *A Stricken Field*'s penultimate chapter, Rita's and the reader's listening in the dark *is* the "scene" of Nazi atrocity.

It is the construction of its readers as historically situated observers, readers who will participate in the text's antifascist work through this contradictory appeal to and withdrawal of vision during the Nazi period, that allows *A Stricken Field* to offer a different analysis of the connections between torture, vision, language, and resistance than the one offered here by Scarry:

> Almost anyone looking at the *physical* act of torture would be immediately appalled and repulsed by the torturers. It is difficult to think of a human situation in which the lines of moral responsibility are more starkly drawn. . . . Yet as soon as the focus of attention shifts to the *verbal* aspect of torture those lines have begun to waver and change their shape in the direction of accommodating and crediting the torturers. (35)

Scarry is referring specifically to two very serious problems in cultural perceptions of torture and the verbal interrogation that almost invariably accompanies it: (1) inadvertently admitting a "motive" for torture in the torturer's claim that the infliction of physical pain is in service of seeking information and (2) inadvertently discrediting a victim of torture who *does* confess and therefore "betray." Scarry rightly claims that "[t]he one is an absolution of responsibility; the other is a conferring of responsibility; the two together turn the moral reality of torture upside down" (35). In Scarry's analysis, this unreflecting perception of interrogation's role in torture, encouraged by any regime that inflicts torture, not only deflects attention away from the central, overwhelming fact of physical pain but also indirectly serves the torturing regime.

If what Scarry claims is true, how can *A Stricken Field*, with its textual absence of the sight of torture, its "scene" of torture consisting almost exclusively of its verbal aspects, work against torture? I would say that it does so through leaving the traces of Rita's vision in the narrative, through those marked absences of and underscored gaps in vision — in other words, through the inscription of *vision under erasure*. The text more effectively represents for its American readers the loss of vision (and control of subjectivity) experienced by the victims of Nazism without running the risk of reproducing the controlling effects of fascist visuality. The text manages, through its contradictory use of vision, to make "visible" but to refuse to specularize the scene of torture, just as it makes visible but refuses to specularize Rita's sexuality. The effect of this refusal to participate in specularization either of sexuality or extreme bodily pain is the text's best way of constructing its readers as antifascist observers.

The novel's last few chapters provide a brief glimpse for its readers of the power of the gaze of state surveillance. Both Rita and Mary are objects within the visual field of "the all-seeing eye of the State," but the differences in their positions under surveillance are important. The last appearance of Rita in the novel is when, after climbing out of the basement of the house in which Peter has just been killed, she sits on a bench near a river. Rita's devastation is troped in terms of vision: "She sat there . . . unmoving, staring ahead, seeing nothing" (275). The remainder of the chapter, about two pages, is narrated from the point of view of the local Czech police officer who finds Rita on the bench:

> He passed . . . and noticed the extra darkness where she was. He came close and spoke and pulled out his flashlight and shone it on her face. . . . By the hair, it was a woman. But where would a woman have come from with a face like that? . . . But it was her eyes that he could not understand. They were wide open and they blinked in the light, they were not blind, but they were as flat, lifeless and hard as stone. (275)

The police officer, finding out that Rita is a German refugee, initiates the procedure that will send her back to Germany by taking her to the local police station. This passage leaves Rita as the unseeing object of official surveillance (a surveillance that will, a reader imagines, be ultimately responsible for her death): "He walked behind her. He wanted to keep his eye on her, to make sure she didn't do anything to get him into trouble" (277). Rita's point of view literally disappears from the novel; she is last seen (both visually and in the narrative) through the policeman's eyes.

Mary is briefly subjected to a version of this kind of policing gaze. At the customs counter at the airport as she is leaving Czechoslovakia, smuggling out in her purse eyewitness narratives of the Nazi invasion (documents attesting to the dangers as well as the importance of vision for the victims of the Third Reich), she sees two men behind the customs officials who did not move or speak. They had looked at all the passengers, slowly, with no expression on their faces and no change in their steady, impersonal eyes. You could see their eyes examining, carefully, feature by feature, each man and woman who stood by the counter. The two men did not shift their positions or take their hands out of their pockets. They were as controlled and quiet as animals, and their unwinking flat eyes were strange to see. . . . She turned away. She did not want to see them. Looking at their eyes and mouths, she could feel a prickle run down her back. . . . She knew their eyes were the real danger in the room. (294–95)

The eyes of government surveillance are the last thing Mary experiences in Czechoslovakia, just as the gaze of the policeman is the last the text tells of Rita. In both cases, the seeing subjects under fascism (both its victims and its agents) are subject to a dehumanization that is recognized in the way they see, by the looks in their eyes. However, the two agents at the airport are described from Mary's point of view, while Rita's point of view, her very ability to see, like Rita herself, has disappeared. That disappearance is known to the readers, but not to Mary, whose point of view frames the novel. The closing paragraph reenacts the opening scene of looking at the same aerial view with which the novel opens: "Mary Douglas stared down at the neat fields. . . . There were the white roads and the white farmhouses and the . . . trees. But the land doesn't look any different, she thought. The land doesn't look any different at all" (302).

The text is framed by Mary's act of looking—a failure of vision that is also a possible recuperation of vision, as the American observer again exercises a kind of visual resistance to the Nazi invasion and its newly imposed boundaries. However, Mary's own lack of knowledge of what has happened to Rita and Peter, her ignorance of what the reader has "seen," renders ironic the text's framing by the gaze of the American female observer and calls into question her ability to adequately "frame," to contain, or to represent (in the sense not only of representation in language but also in the political sense, to speak for) the brutalizing of vision, bodies, and subjectivity under fascism. When the refugees in the novel attempt to represent themselves in language, through the telling and transcribing of eyewitness narratives, their ability to do so is undercut by the mediation of official "observers," journalists like Mary who are in turn subject to restrictions on what they can represent. The eyewitness narratives that Mary carries out of the country are themselves signs of the questioning to which vision-represented-in-language is subject in this novel. Reading over the narratives in her hotel room, Mary both acknowledges the enormous importance and "power of two or three typewritten pages that tell the truth" (285) and questions how they will be read or "used" by readers outside the Third Reich: "if I called in . . . everybody and let them make copies, they couldn't use it. I can't use it. We wouldn't be believed. We'd be accused of propaganda, the way we always are" (287).

Like the medieval chronicles that Hayden White analyzes and that the novel's epigraphs invoke, *A Stricken Field* "breaks off *in medias res*, in the chronicler's own present; it leaves things unresolved" (White 5). The dual sense of the power and "uselessness" of eyewitness narratives indirectly gestures toward the novel's readers' ability and willingness not only to imagine the sight of others but to engage with and possibly respond to the language of others. Referring to the work of organizations such as Amnesty International, Elaine Scarry has written that the person who "use[s] language to let pain give an accurate account of itself . . . willingly turns himself into an image of the other's psychic or sentient claims, an image existing in the space outside the sufferer's body" (50). My sense is that by picturing the "downcast eyes" of the female observer and victim of Nazi occupation policies, *A Sticken Field* might be read as accomplishing a similar goal for an American readership on the verge of entering World War II.

4

Vision, Violence, and *Vogue*: War and Correspondence in Lee Miller's Photography

HIS CHAPTER WILL LOOK AT LEE MILLER'S WAR CORRESPON-
dence and photography for *Vogue* magazine in order to explore how she
constructed herself and her predominantly female audience as observers of the "European theater of operations" (*Lee Miller's War* 203) and
of the most extreme effects of Nazi ideology, the concentration camps at
Dachau and Buchenwald. Miller's wartime photographs can, I think, best
be understood as working both with and against some of the conventions
of surrealist and fashion photography, genres to which her work was closely
connected and that formed a nexus for the construction of the wartime female subject for Miller as an artist and for her female audience. A primary
concern in reading and viewing Miller's war correspondence is, indeed,
correspondence — not only between her work and these other visual discourses, but also between subject and object, in the complex interplay be-

tween the female viewer and the represented human figures who can be read as both seeing subjects and visual objects in her photographs.

As we have seen in chapter 2, Jacobus suggests that the textual model of letters rests on an interplay of identity and difference between correspondents. My aim is to explore how Miller's representations of bodies and spaces during the war evoke, dismantle, and rearrange the specular subject-object relations central to surrealist, fashion, and combat photography and, in more extreme and physically threatening form, to fascist ideology. Miller's photographs establish for her *Vogue* audience the possibility of a correspondence, but it is an often tense, difficult, and contradictory interplay of identity and difference between seeing subject and visual object. This correspondence is centrally concerned with the perception of the gendered body and the gendered viewer as they are affected by the war and by the most extreme effects of Nazism: by the radical damage done to bodies and the complex ways that damage is kept in view.

As I will explore in more detail below, specularity, with its insistence on unified subjectivity and a unified field of perception, provides a model of visual experience that is crucial to the four discourses with which this essay and Miller's photography are most concerned: surrealist and fashion photography, which both seek to eliminate the distance and difference between image and viewer; war photography, which like other kinds of wartime discourse attempts to create a unified, national subject that will support military objectives and homefront sacrifices; fascist aesthetics and ideology, characterized by their "obsession with both difference and sameness" (Mizejewski 32) and which, as we have seen in chapter 3, can be in part understood as grotesque extremes of specular thought, as "the specularization of social, sexual, and political life" (Elsaesser 548).

Miller's case is an especially valuable one for exploring the diverse set of discourses for the construction of the female subject in the war and prewar years because of her own participation as a model and as a photographer in French surrealism and in the New York fashion industry of the late 1920s and mid-1930s. Born in Poughkeepsie in 1907, Miller worked as a fashion model in New York and was photographed by Edward Steichen, among others, for Condé Nast publications. She went to Paris in 1929, lived with the photographer Man Ray, working as his model and as a photographer and exhibiting her work in Paris galleries. In 1932, she returned to New York and opened a photography studio with her brother. In 1934, she married an Egyptian businessman, living with him in Egypt and Europe. She eventually separated from him to live in London with the British writer and surrealist artist Roland Penrose. She became a member of the British *Vogue* staff in 1940 and was British and American *Vogue*'s European correspondent in 1944 and 1945.[1]

Miller's relation to photography was, in other words, that of both seer and seen, as she worked on both sides of the camera within cultural moments and milieus that were concerned with representing the female body—either for a male or a female viewer—and with collapsing the distance between the seeing subject and its visual object. Before looking at Miller's wartime photographs (including her fashion shots taken immediately after the liberation of Paris), I want to explore her work with the surrealists. This exploration will, I hope, prove valuable for what it can reveal about subject/object relations or correspondences, especially as set in motion by the representation of the gendered body—issues crucial to Miller's work during the war.

Disarming Surrealism

> First and foremost, surrealism teaches relations and the art of interacting.
>
> — MARY ANN CAWS, *The Art of Interference*

Miller's work with the surrealists as model and photographer—the oscillation between seeing and being seen, between functioning as an icon and as a constructor of vision, representing and being represented—makes the photographic work in which she participated well suited to exploring surrealist aesthetics and its problematic relation to gendered subjectivity and the representation of the female body. I want to juxtapose my reading of one of Miller's surrealist photographs with some influential claims about surrealist aesthetics and the representation of the female body made by Mary Ann Caws and Rosalind Krauss. What particularly interests me in the work of these two critics is that both discuss Man Ray photographs of Miller in order to explore a crucial element of surrealist aesthetics: the loss of boundaries and the uneasy union of opposites. Their claims about this aspect of surrealism and their illustrative use of the Man Ray images of Miller, alongside my reading of one of Miller's own surrealist photographs, will help to clarify Miller's peculiar position within surrealism and the kind of correspondence or play of difference her photography established and extended in her later wartime photography.

Many commentators on surrealist aesthetics have discussed the movement's desire to juxtapose opposing or different objects and values, to break down binary oppositions through the "coupling of irreconcilable realities" (Stich 11).[2] This agenda affected the act of seeing itself for the surrealists. Caws writes that central to the agenda of surrealist visuality was the ideal of conflating or joining the seeing subject and its object, an overcoming of "the split between visionary and view" (112). Along with other feminist theorists and critics of surrealism, Caws expresses a deep suspicion of this specularizing desire to unify seer and seen when the surrealist visual object is the female body, claiming that such images tend to provide "no role except enforced submission" for the pictured woman: the image "is a one-way venture, far from the erotics of exchange, open only to a willing relation of dominator and dominated" (119).[3] This dynamic implicates as well the female viewer, who "is—willingly or not, partially or wholly—identified with the body under observation" (112).

Caws briefly examines as one example of this aspect of surrealist visuality a Man Ray photograph of Lee Miller, identified only as "a live female model," wearing "a wire mesh hat" that covers her head, face, and neck almost completely, save for an opening on one side that reveals the left ear and some hair (plate 7). Caws characterizes the image as one of "female entrapment" and "submission to . . . netting and . . . capture." Miller, looking out at the viewer from the enclosing wire mesh grid, is described as "a prey who is rendered simultaneously mute and speaking of objecthood" (114).

I agree with Caws's reading of the image, which she places next to other surrealist images of female entrapment that invite (or, rather, demand) the female viewer to occupy either a position of submission along with the model or a position of complicity with the dominating gaze of the male photographer. However, taking up in a somewhat different way the surrealist attention to relations and interactions, I want to set this photograph next to one taken by Miller herself in order to see how in her early photography she might be participating in a dialogue of dissent with her surrealist mentor over representing the female body and over the distance or proximity between subject and object. Her "Nude with a Wire Mesh Sabre Guard" (plate 8), taken in 1930, the same year as the Man Ray photograph, also uses the same prop, the wire mesh, now placed on the left arm and shoulder of a female model, who is seen in profile, her neck slightly arched, her eyes looking up, her shoulder-length hair brushing and covering a piece of the mesh at the shoulder. Like the Man Ray photograph, the wire mesh occupies the place of an article of clothing, but here, the metallic object seems to be worn lightly, like a cloak draped on one shoulder. It follows the curve of the model's shoulder, arm, and breast, whereas in the Man Ray photograph, the wire mesh "hat" imposes, or rather superimposes, its own shape on Miller's head. Is the female body, so well fitted with this sabre guard, then, a weapon, rather than a prey? My sense is rather that the object that speaks of capture in the Man Ray photograph is now something that actually speaks more of potentially free movement, both for the model, understood as the representation of subjectivity, and for the viewer of the photograph. The angle of the woman's head and face direct the line of sight out of and away from the mesh, almost as if the mesh were some shell or carapace about to be shed or a cloak about to be dropped. Miller's photograph evokes not a visual vocabulary of capture or threat but rather a disarming of the viewer posited by the Man Ray image. The wire mesh on the woman's shoulder and arm could be said to reinscribe the distance between seer and seen that surrealism sought to collapse. The wire mesh, though permeable and partial (perhaps because it is permeable and partial), is also a shield, a visual interruption for the viewer that leaves both the viewer and the pictured woman unencumbered, constituted in and by difference.

This appropriation of what in a different visual context is a constraint, rendering it a fitting garment easily shed or a shield lightly worn, establishes one version of a surrealist image that allows liberatory possibilities to the female subject imagined on either side of the lens. Caws finds a slightly different version of surrealist juxtaposition most inviting for the female subject: "the free exchange of the ideas of possible images" (127)—in other words, a kind of correspondence, the union not of viewer and object but rather of disparate objects within the frame of the photograph, such as the human body with nature. One of Caws's examples of such a surrealist practice is an untitled Man Ray photograph of, again, Lee Miller (plate 9), representing a female torso near a window, the skin surface marked, seemingly imprinted, by shadows from a translucent curtain. Caws writes that in this photograph, the body is not deformed, but rather "one object is . . . augmented by the other and each rendered more interesting: their union is not forced but imaginative, and multiple in its possibilities" (127).

This Man Ray photograph of Miller's torso by the window, along with a variation of it in which the photo is not cropped at the neck but instead includes Miller's face (plate 10), and which constitutes part of a triptych of Miller standing by a window, are the very photographs that Rosalind Krauss uses as primary examples of the surrealist fascination with, what she terms, "mimicry," after the work of the surrealist writer and sociologist Roger Caillois.[4] Caillois studied the ways in which animals camouflage themselves, "mimicking" their surroundings, not so much as an act of self-protection but as a kind of "psychosis." If the existence of an individual creature is based on its "self-possession" or distinctness, mimicry signifies the loss of distinctness, because in the act of self-camouflaging, the animal merges with its environment, becoming "dispossessed, derealized, as though yielding to a temptation exercised on it by the vast outsideness of space itself, a temptation to fusion" (Krauss, "Corpus Delicti" 74). Caillois used the phenomenon of animal mimicry as a metaphor for schizophrenia in humans, but Krauss sees the achieving or at least the representation of this loss of corporeal boundaries as one of the aims of surrealist visual practice, best embodied by these Man Ray photographs of Miller, which demonstrate "the inscription of space on the body of an organism" ("Corpus Delicti" 74).

For Caws, the Man Ray photographs of Miller that represent the collapse of boundaries and the union of opposites also map two polar positions of the female body (and the relationship of the female viewer of that body) within surrealism: that of dominated object and that of potential liberation. Krauss's position falls between, or, perhaps, outside, these poles: the loss of boundaries involved in mimicry carries not so much a political as a psychoanalytic charge. However, for both Caws and Krauss, the convergence pictured in these Man Ray images of Lee Miller—and the dynamics of Miller's own photograph — suggests an understanding of the surrealist construction of subjectivity as an oscillating, complex relationship between subject and object, viewer and viewed, a relationship based on what I have been calling correspondence.

The issues raised by this brief look at Miller's participation in the surrealist movement—the ideal of diminishing or erasing the distance between subject and object, the possibilities of inscribing a seeing subject constituted by both identity and difference, the gendered body open to the erasure of boundaries and inscription by the space surrounding it, the liberating or dispossessing effects of such an erasure, the struggles of the female observer to find a position that is neither complicitous with nor submissive to a dominating gaze—all surface with new and often irresolvable tensions in Miller's wartime photography. In representing human figures during the war, human figures who are in some of these reports in extremes of imaginable pain or brutalization or victims of the worst of Nazi atrocities, Miller's photographs constantly experimented with the positioning and constructing of a wartime subject within and outside the photograph's frame. Her work shows an abiding concern with distance and proximity, identification and difference, the unstable relation of figure to ground, in order to inscribe a female viewer who would as far as possible take into account the enormous damage of war to the human body. As Elaine Scarry has suggested, "the main purpose and outcome of war is injuring" and this fact "can disappear from view along many separate paths" (63–64).[5] One of the projects of Miller's work was to make and keep that view possible through an attention to the complexities of subject-object relations and to the gendered body in conflict.

Equally important for our understanding of Miller's work and of how she might have attempted to construct herself and her *Vogue* audience as observers of war are her 1944 posed "fashion" photographs, which I would like to examine next. These photographs are of interest not only for how they disrupt the conventions of fashion discourse but also for how they establish visual parameters of proximity and distance for Miller's later photographs of the war.

The Pattern of Liberation, Or, Fashioning Distance

> Is there some way of looking that is not the look of an intruder, some interpretation from which we could exempt ourselves as consumers?
>
> — MARY ANN CAWS, *The Art of Interference*

> The pattern of liberation isn't very decorative.
>
> — LEE MILLER, *Lee Miller's War*

The feminist suspicion of the surrealist desire to collapse subject/object boundary lines seems particularly well warranted if we consider another set of discourses, more or less coeval with surrealism, that also aimed to produce such a collapse: women's fashion magazines and "the woman's film" of the 1930s and 1940s. Feminist film theorists, most notably Mary Anne Doane, studying the woman's film of the 1940s discuss how the genre constructs a female viewing subject in whom the distance between subject and object is radically diminished. For the female spectator addressed by these films, seeing, appearing, being, and having were conflated in the perception of the female star and her material surroundings, which constitute the "image/commodity" on the screen (Doane 177). As Doane and other feminist historians have observed, the period of World War II marked "a crisis point in the elaboration of female subjectivity" (Doane 178): the U.S. government actively recruited women for jobs historically held by men and encouraged homefront economies and sacrifices, while at the same time cultural apparatus such as film and magazines continually reinscribed women's roles as consumers of fashionable goods, despite wartime commodities shortages.[6]

One method of cultural management of such a crisis was the insistent inscription of pathos — intense (over)identification between text and spectator — in women's film genres. For Doane, pathos always involves a loss of individual subjectivity and "is thus one way of containing the potentially disruptive effects of attributing the gaze to the woman, of delineating a specifically female subjectivity" (178). Doane claims that for female viewers of women's films, the cinematic image "is both shop window and mirror," a site where the viewer's subjectivity and objectification are conflated (33). Another site of such pathos — the specular collapse of seeing subject with the visual object of desire — is, of course, women's fashion magazines.[7]

It is within just such a context — *Vogue* magazine — that Miller's war correspondence and many of her extraordinary photographs were published. Miller's images of the war both set up and dismantled the *Vogue* image/commodity machine as they reinscribed the distance between the subject and object that surrealist texts and the visual products of the fashion industry sought to efface. If, as Mikhail Bakhtin claimed, in pathos "there is no distance, there are no reservations" (qtd. in Doane 177), Miller kept, and encouraged her *Vogue* audience to keep, what Man Ray had inscribed on the reverse of a photograph of one of Miller's eyes: "an eye always in reserve" (qtd. in Livingston, *Lee Miller: Photographer* 40).

Miller's documentary piece on the liberation of Paris as it appeared in *Vogue* in November 1944 is perhaps most striking for the conflict between Miller's own text and the editor's captions for her photographs. Next to images of the Place de la Concorde seen through barbed wire barricades are several photographs whose captions draw the reader's and viewer's attention to the dresses and hairstyles of the women pictured: "Made for cycling — rayon dress with apron front"; "French girls go in for long Veronica Lake hair-do's" (Miller, "Paris" 95). In the text of Miller's report, women's dresses and hairstyles are described and understood as political gestures: the women "had all deliberately organized this style of dressing and living as a taunt to the Huns. . . . Saving material and labor meant help to the Germans — and it was their duty to waste instead of save" (*Lee Miller's War* 69).[8]

I am even more interested here in the photographs not published in Miller's piece on the liberation of Paris, posed fashion photos that were in fact sharply criticized by the magazine's American editor, Edna Woolman Chase, and that both would evoke and disrupt, through inscribing distance between the viewer and the model, the image/commodity mechanism so crucial to fashion discourse.[9] According to a telegram sent to Miller by her British editor, "Edna critical . . . especially cheap mannequins urges more elegance . . . + wellbred women. . . . Edna says quote can't believe pictures typical of highclass french fashion. . . . can't Solange get ladies to pose unquote" (*Lee Miller's War* 80). In her letter of reply, Miller shifts the argument away from the class terms with which Chase categorizes the female body photographed for commercial consumption:

> These snap shots have been taken under the most difficult and depressing conditions. . . . Edna should be told that maybe there's a war on — that maybe Solange hasn't the heart to concentrate with the knowledge of the horrors her husband and family are going through in German prison camps. (*Lee Miller's War* 84)

However, the photographs themselves are even more politicized and disruptive of the pathos-inducing conventions of fashion photography through their use of distancing and visual interferences between the viewer and the model. Two images (plates 11 and 12) identified by Miller's caption sheets as posed fashion shots ("Paquin's navy-blue woolen dress, Place de la Concorde"; "Bruyère's quilted windbreaker, Place Vendôme" [*Lee Miller's War* 83–84]) actually establish as objects of scrutiny the disappearance or, rather, the absorption of the models and their costumes into their surroundings. The shot taken at the Place de la Concorde situates the model at such a distance from the camera (which is on the other side of the basin of a fountain) that she is almost lost between the sculpture in the foreground and the large buildings in the background. She is so far away that she appears to be mostly a miniature mass of dark and light: her pale head, legs, and hands and the set of wavy white stripes contrast strongly with and almost seem to separate from the dark dress. She is both fragmented by the dark and light that represent her body and overwhelmed by exterior objects. Far more noticeable are the fountain statues, particularly the discolored and muddied female figure in the left foreground.

The photograph in the Place Vendôme is taken from inside the entrance foyer of a building (a plaque to the left of the door identifies one occupant as the designer Bruyère). The model standing outside is framed by a large glass double door, one side of which is open. The pane of glass in the closed half of the door is evidently full of bullet holes, for it is badly cracked, and there are eight large rectangular patches of tape covering holes in the glass. Whereas in the previous photo, the model seems divided and fragmented by extremes of dark and light seen from a distance, this shot is remarkably lacking in contrast. The woman's face, swathed in a hood, is shadowed and dim. Her gloved hands almost disappear in the folds and shadows of her jacket. The skirt casts a shadow on her legs, rendering them the same color as the rest of her figure.

With the women seeming to disappear inside their clothes or into the built environment, these photographs recall the mimicry, the erasure of boundaries between figure and environment, so notable in the Man Ray photographs of Miller. However, these fashion photographs, which should induce the process of identification or dissolution of visual boundaries in its viewers, put that loss of boundaries at such a distance from the viewer that the erasure of boundaries is itself the object of scrutiny. The photographs furthermore fill the visual field between viewer and model with marks of physical decay and destruction, traces of disruption and difference, which in the second photograph are the clear traces of the war recently fought.

Even when Miller's camera moves closer to the fashion model, the female figures are protected inside of their surroundings and shielded from the female viewer and the act of identification. In "Models relaxing before a fashion show" (plate 13; *Lee Miller's War* 82–83), three women are pictured wrapped in blankets from the waist down, lying on the floor, their heads resting on overturned chairs. The legs of the chairs protrude like muzzles of rifles above the women's heads. The face of the woman closest to the camera is completely hidden behind a newspaper; the second reads a book, her eyes on the page; the third looks at the camera, but one eye is effaced by a protruding chair leg. Even though relatively close to the camera, these women are inaccessible to the viewer, protected by the wrapping, the newspaper, and the gun-like shapes above their heads. Along the curtained wall to the right of the three women is a table holding several hats that range from a canister-like shape on a small hat-stand to a shapeless mass of fur resting on the table's surface. The photograph pictures the fragmentation of fashion photography down to some of its constituent forms (now rendered shapeless or decontextualized, separated from the female body), while the models are protected from and inaccessible to full view.

In these three photographs, Miller is picturing not only fashion models (usually the objects of over-identification for *Vogue* readers) but, in her distancing from these female figures who are partially absorbed back into their surroundings, is actually picturing the tension of correspondence for female viewers of female figures, the tension between (over)identification with the image and the distancing and fragmentation of that image, a tension that puts a significant strain of the specular workings of the image/commodity machine.

Another photograph, showing uniformed U.S. servicewomen at a fashion show (plate 14), is both a close-up view of the image/commodity mechanism at work and a strain on that mechanism. The seated women are so close to the model standing in their midst that they can and do touch the fabric of the dress, their arms and hands following the trajectory of their eyes, which are all intensely focused on the dress itself, even though the model is looking directly down at the face of one of the women examining the dress, as if to engage her in conversation. Here, the act of looking, of engaging in identification rather than in dialogue with the female object, is itself the object of sight. This, I suggest, creates a rift between the viewers *of* the photographs and the viewers pictured *in* it. The model's dark head is well above those of the seated servicewomen and is set sharply against a light-colored door in the background. She is wearing a close-fitting plaid dress with a strongly contrasting light and dark pattern; the effect for the viewer of the photograph is that her head and legs appear visually separate from the plaid torso. Like the model at the fountain in the Place de la Concorde, her body is fragmented into separate zones, making the viewer's identification with a whole image nearly impossible. With their gaze following a very focused trajectory, emphasized by arms and hands, the only part of the model that seems to exist visually for the servicewomen is the plaid torso, while the viewer's eyes are drawn both to the fragmented vertical line of the model's body and to the horizontal line of the women viewers in uniform. While the women in uniform are fixed by their own uniform gaze at the image/commodity, the photograph's viewer is offered a more mobile and contradictory glance over the visual field.[10]

The distances, interruptions, and schisms produced by these photographs would certainly help to undermine the loss of subject-object boundaries, which is the goal of fashion photography. Miller's fashion shots for her piece on liberated Paris could be said to liberate her potential viewers from the closed, uniform circuit of identification with the image/commodity, underlining the crisis in wartime female subjectivity that

Doane describes. These photographs use the place held open by the suspension of that identification for inscribing difference, which is a central element in the representations of the wounded male body that constitute much of the later images in Miller's wartime work.

Broken Views of Allied Bodies

In Miller's photographs of Allied troops at or near the front in August 1944, as in most of wartime photography, it is predominantly male bodies in danger, wounded, or dead that are represented. It is important to note, however, that in her representation of the wounded Allied soldier, Miller's work is remarkably restrained when compared to the representations of wounded Allies found at this point in the war in the work of other photojournalists working for American publications such as *Life*. The first image of an American soldier's corpse appeared in the American press in August 1943 (Moeller 224); photographs of combat dead and wounded grew gradually more explicit throughout the last two years of the war, although photographs containing images of American soldiers' blood did not appear until 1945 (Moeller 224, 227; Roeder 1). According to Susan Moeller and George Roeder, the increasingly graphic depiction of injured or dead American soldiers in the last two years of the war was aimed, in overtly articulated government policy, at reducing civilian complacency over the outcome of the war, producing a greater agreement with homefront sacrifices such as rationing and wage controls, and improving morale.[11] Another way to understand the propagandistic use of the wounded or dead American soldier's image is in terms of pathos. In many of the images of the wounded soldier prevalent in the popular and women's press in the later years of the war, pathos, an eliciting of the female viewer's over-identification and empathy, was turned not into economic activity but rather an acceptance of wartime economic restrictions.

What I characterized above as Miller's restraint in the representation of wounded soldiers must be understood in this historical context: increasingly graphic representations of dead American soldiers in the final two years of the war were used as some of the primary visual material of government propaganda, for social and economic manipulation and control of civilians, in many cases particularly female civilians. Keeping in mind

Scarry's claim that the central fact of war's damage to the body can "disappear from view along many separate paths" (63–64), it can be said that the increasingly focused propagandistic look at the damage done to male bodies late in the war was actually one of the paths by which the central fact of injuring "disappeared" before the very eyes of American observers. The images of these dead soldiers—and the verbal discourses surrounding them—worked finally to focus civilian attention on homefront activity, rather than to remain on the physical pain and destruction of bodies in Europe and Asia.

I am interested in how Miller's visual strategies of fragmenting and distancing of the injured soldier's body can actually act against such a disappearance, and against the kind of propagandistic work performed by much wartime photography. I want to look here at Miller's first overseas piece for *Vogue* to examine how her representation of the wounded Allied soldier, like her shots of the models in Paris, both evoke and resist photographic conventions in their construction of their female readers/viewers as wartime subjects. Miller's work is, at least at this point in her overseas career, concerned with constructing her viewers without recourse to more commonly recognized visual vocabularies that constituted part of the United States's war propaganda program. Miller's photographs tend to undermine the model of subjectivity most readily inscribed by propagandistic discourse: the subject of the "whole picture," a specularized seeing subject constituted by a unified view of the war. Miller's photographs work, I suggest, to construct the female wartime observer neither as a unified subject of propaganda nor as a disappearing subject of pathos (two models of specular thought and vision that can be understood as closely related) but rather as a subject open to rifts, schisms, and difference—and one who thus keeps in view the central fact of the wounded body. It is in this questioning of the unified subject of vision, too, that Miller's work registers a certain ambivalence about her own photographic authority, one that resonates with the early lessons of surrealism.

In Miller's photographs of an American tent hospital in the newly liberated France of August 1944, the wounded bodies of soldiers are surrounded and fragmented by equipment or people, by the arms of doctors or nurses, and by tent ropes, tubes, and bandages. Finally, they are fragmented by the look of the female viewer, who is herself fragmented, unseated from a location of unifying and unified visual authority. In some photos, it seems that the wounded body is a field for its own visual interruption and fragmentation. A photograph of a "surgeon using bronchoscope" (plate 15; *Lee Miller's War* 28) is a good example. What is visible of the soldier-patient is a side view of his upper torso, his left arm from forearm to shoulder, and his neck and chin. Most striking about the shot is that it is not really the soldier's body that is the focus, but, as the caption suggests, the bronchoscope (a metal cylinder in the center of the photo), the surgeons's hand holding the scope, and the surgeon himself. The bronchoscope seems like an extension of the surgeon's arm, which allows the eye to follow it, unbroken, back up to the face of the surgeon, who is looking through the scope, whose function is unclear to the viewer. The surgeon's hand, holding the scope at an angle, interrupts a full view of the lower part of the soldier's face, so it is unclear how exactly the tube relates to the soldier's body. Moreover, what the surgeon sees through the scope is a realm of vision unavailable to the viewer. The fragmenting of the view is exacerbated further by four other medical personnel in the shot, all looking in different directions, all providing possible, conflicting trajectories of sight for the photograph's viewer to follow. The nurse behind the doctor is looking at him; of the two men toward the soldier's feet, one is looking at the soldier (clearly an angle we cannot share because he is looking from above), and the other is looking at his fellow medic's hand, which is another element that blocks and fragments the soldier's body. The other figure in the photograph, the nurse standing on the left side, has her eyes closed. There is also a tube resting on the soldier's shoulder, seeming to separate his arm from the rest of his body. This representation of the act of looking at and into a soldier's body, looking closely at the damage done by combat, is for the viewer an experience of visual distance, fragmentation and blockage, even as the soldier himself, ostensibly the "focus" of the photograph, is fragmented and absorbed by his surroundings.

Another photo, an unfocused close-up of the torso of a man whose head, face, chest and hands are completely wrapped in bandages and occupying fully the first page of the *Vogue* article, offers another site for both distancing and fragmenting the seeing subject of wartime photography (plate 16; *Lee Miller's War* 18–19; *Vogue* September 1944, 138). Miller's comment in the text (also published in the *Vogue* article as the caption for the photograph) is: "A bad burn case asked me to take his picture as he wanted to see how funny he looked. It was pretty grim, and I didn't focus well." According to the caption, then, the photo is taken for the soldier himself, for his own eyes to look at (at least potentially), an image made for self-reflection. The photo, read with the caption, fragments and disperses its viewers among several seeing positions, or, to put it another way, points simultaneously to several different locations for the seeing subject: that of (1) the photographer, (2) the *Vogue* reader/viewer, and (3) the self-reflecting object of the view, the wounded soldier. I want to explore each of these positions a bit more closely.

With its blurred focus, the photograph draws attention to the physical situation of the photographer and the act of photographing itself. It is, in other words, deictic, an image that leaves traces of the moment of its making, gesturing back to the physical presence of the artist.[12] The photograph also makes visible the possibility of swerving, of not looking straight, of a mechanical and human looking-askance. The act of looking and picturing — or of looking askance and of mis-picturing — is being made visible, inserted or dropped like a curtain in between the viewer and the soldier. It is, in this sense, a photograph of Miller's subject-position, mediated by the camera, the lens, the photographic apparatus that represents not only the soldier but also the photographer's response to his grim image. It is not perhaps so much that Miller refused to look but rather that she refused to represent "clearly" and thereby underlined the very act of representing, the construction of the image that most photographs would have read as "natural." It is in this way that the image's lack of focus actually holds the fact of wounding more clearly "in view," in Scarry's sense of the term. The extreme and hidden disfigurement of the soldier's body, its movement away from its "natural" unwounded state by the burn, is both hidden and emphasized by the bandages. The blurred focus pulls the fact of disfigurement even further into the visual foreground or rather inserts it between foreground and viewer. The wounded male body is triply distanced from the "natural" through the denaturing or blurring of the photographic image itself.

The blurred focus of this photograph thus also calls up the issue of photographic authority, an issue doubly important for a female photographer working so close to combat zones, and one whose work, as I have suggested, ran counter to the propagandistic uses of images of the male body in physical extremity. Edward Weston's influential notions of photographic authority suggest that the power of a photograph is based on a "quality of authenticity" that leads the viewer to believe that "he would have seen that scene or object exactly so if he had been there" (qtd. in Krauss, "Corpus Delicti" 91). Krauss comments that this kind of photographic authority "is grounded in the sharply focused image, its resolution a figure of the unity of what the spectator sees, a wholeness that in turn founds the spectator himself as a unified subject. That subject . . . seems to find unbearable a photograph that effaces categories" ("Corpus Delicti" 95). In the photograph of the burn case, the particular photograph's, photographer's, and viewer's authority is put into question, along with the larger notion of wartime photographic "authority." A similar questioning of visual authority and, concomitantly, the unity of the viewing subject, was enabled by surrealist photography, which, according to Krauss "does not admit of the natural, as opposed to the cultural or made, and so all of what it looks at is seen as if already, and always, constructed. . . . The object, 'straight' or manipulated, is always manipulated" ("Corpus Delicti" 91). Through emphasizing the constructed nature of the photographic image, Miller also emphasizes the altering of the wounded male body and the unstable position of the photograph's viewer.

That viewer, the *Vogue* reader, looks at a blurred photo of white bandages, a barely recognizable human form looking back at the camera. The viewer is herself split, since the photo undermines standard notions of photographic authority, inviting, perhaps even requiring, the viewer to ask herself if she would see the same thing, the same way, if she had been there. The blurred focus would seem to say no, calling into question the photograph's authority, separating the photographer and viewer: "Were I there, I would see it clearly." Yet, the photograph might also evoke a hesitation, a set of doubtful questions for its viewer: Would she really see clearly? Would she look? Is this blurring an image of her own need or desire to look askance on the wounded male body and the fact of the deep injuriousness of war? The blurring makes this questioning possible, in fact calls for it. The undermined authority of the photograph and photographer creates schisms for and in the *Vogue* viewer: rifts between her and the photographer, in her own ways of seeing (would I focus or refuse to focus; would I look or look away?), and as Krauss suggests, in her very situation as a unified subject.

A final rift in the visual field stems from the fact that the photograph seen with its caption invites the viewer to imagine the soldier looking back at his own image. The potentially reflecting subject (seeing a blurred image of himself wrapped in bandages) is both seer and picture. He is made strange, altered, transformed by the lack of focus, which calls attention to the act of representing, and by the bandages, which hide the wounds that will in all likelihood be permanently disfiguring.

This photograph of the burned and bandaged soldier imagined to be looking at his own image calls forth an extreme version of the Lacanian subject of vision, dispossessed not only by the visual field in which he is both seer and seen but by the wounds he has received and by the very representation of those wounds. Krauss claims that when a viewer looks at a photograph of her or himself "there is a fundamental schism between the subject that perceives and the image that looks back at him, because the image, in which he is captured, is seen from the vantage of another" ("Corpus Delicti" 78) and that surrealist photography tends to exploit this schism more than other photographic traditions. In the photograph of the badly burned soldier, it is his status as a wounded soldier that, in the first place, places him as an object of his own and others' vision and that hides, disfigures, and renders him inaccessible to any whole vision, including his own. If one is to "hold steadily visible the centrality of injuring" (Scarry 336), one is more and more drawn into the realm of the alienated, split subject of vision and away from the specular structures of "unity" and "wholeness."

Opposite the burn-case photo in *Vogue* is a small photograph of Miller wearing a helmet with the false eye-visor painted on it. It is the first representation in *Vogue* of Miller herself in her role as war correspondent, and it is a significant one, visually echoing or shadowing the patterns of contradictions and splits that I have discussed above. The visored helmet would signal both accessibility to sight and protection from harm. But with the eyeholes painted on "for fun" (as the caption says), the visor is a joke, a camouflage, a mimicry of safety and sight. The photo is a sign of Miller's status as a female war photographer: like the photographs she takes, the painted visor both invokes and blocks wartime vision, both protects and disarms.

These photographs of injured soldiers, through their simultaneous engagement and disengagement of vision, their acts of visual distancing, blockage, and fragmentation, actually work against the disappearance of some of the most brutal and central effects of the war. In doing so, these images question the authority of vision and the unity both of the view and the viewer of war, a specular unity so often invoked by wartime propaganda as well as by the image/commodity mechanism of *Vogue*. This unified subject is perhaps most radically undermined in the photographs Miller took inside of concentration camps, to which I now want to turn.

Framing the Holocaust

The wounding and wounded that Miller does picture in a far more direct way are in her most disturbing and extreme images of the central fact of war's damage to the human body: those of the concentration camp victims at Dachau and Buchenwald and of the camp guards who were beaten or killed by prisoners after liberation. In both cases, Miller abandons the distancing, fragmenting, and blocking that she used to inscribe a politicized female observer in other moments of the war. The problem facing Miller and her viewers seems to have been how to frame, in both the photographic and conceptual sense of the word, this overwhelming visual evidence of fascism's Final Solution. In the first set of photographs, Miller uses close-ups that seem to abandon as far as possible the notion of framing; while in the photographs of the prison guards, the central figures are intensely and heavily framed and enclosed. Like other photographs in Miller's oeuvre, these are centrally concerned with the dynamics of correspondence, of identification and difference, proximity and distance. However, these photographs intensify these dynamics in such a way that the observer's very subjectivity and humanity seem to be at stake in her visual encounter with these images.

The photographs of "bodies stacked in the courtyard of the crematorium because they had run out of coal the last five days" (*Lee Miller's War* 163) are close-up, clearly focused images with virtually no space between the figures of the bodies and the frame (plate 17). The corpses occupy completely the field of vision, leaving no space of escape or relief for the viewer's line of sight, eliminating distance from what must have evoked (and certainly still does evoke) reflexes of revulsion, of looking away, of disbelief, and a desire to distance.

Miller's textual accompaniments to the photographs acknowledge the possibility, perhaps the inevitability, of such a response. The title of the *Vogue* piece on the camps is a quote from Miller's cable to her editors: "'Believe It'"; according to Miller's biographer Antony Penrose, Miller cabled along with the photographs to her British editor, "I implore you to believe this is true" (139). In one photograph (plate 18), Miller represents the response of disbelief and distancing in military observers. Penrose identifies this as a photograph of "United States medics from Rainbow Company with a dead prisoner at Dachau, 30 April 1945" and writes that "Some of the troops . . . thought the camp a . . . propaganda stunt faked by their own side" (140).[13] The photograph is taken from the inside of a truck, looking outward. On the floor of the truck the head and upper torso of a decimated, clearly starved corpse occupy the left bottom corner of the foreground. Framed by the opening of the truck are the two medics, both with their arms tightly folded across their chests and gazing intently at the dead prisoner. It is a picture not only of a Holocaust victim but of American observers' looking and disbelieving. It represents being caught as an observer within the frame of proximity to incomprehensible damage and at the same time straining against that frame, attempting to insert distance between seer and seen.

Even as Miller must implore her editor and viewers to believe the evidence in these photographs of Nazi extermination policies, her photographs of S.S. guards beaten or killed by their ex-prisoners call into question the reliability of visual images without the crucial verbal framing of the narrative of the Holocaust. The guards are not immediately recognizable as such but are, at first glance, simply beaten men or corpses in civilian clothes, objects of potential identification, pity, or pathos, impulses that must be countered by the viewer's knowledge of the Holocaust, gained from the written text of Miller's report and from the photographs of the massed corpses of these guards' victims. Her report emphasizes that the guards deliberately disguised themselves as civilians when the camps were liberated (*Lee Miller's War* 165), underlining the problem of the reliability of the visual within the confines of the fascist state, a problem that Miller introduces in the opening of her report on the defeat of Germany, noting that the civilians are "all just like real people. But they aren't. They are the enemy" (*Lee Miller's War* 161).

And yet, despite her verbal assertions that the Germans are not "real people," Miller visually holds her viewers to a full mutual gaze with the camp guards. Two shots in particular use strategies drastically different from the distancing, fragmenting, and blocking important in so many of Miller's wartime photographs. Both are fairly close-up images of badly beaten prison guards (identifiable as guards only by the captions), and both rely heavily on double and even triple framing to enclose the guards and the viewer within the visual field. In one (plate 19), a man pictured from the chest up and occupying most of the frame looks directly into the camera, his bloodied face and shirtfront pale and starkly illuminated by a flashbulb. In the dark background is a series of frames within the photographic frame: a square archway enclosing the lower half of a window situated above a radiator. The thin line of window-glass at the very top of the photograph's frame reflects light back at the viewer, and the vertical lines of a radiator form the background for the top of the guard's head. The second shot (plate 20), which was published in *Vogue* (June 1945, 106), is of two beaten guards kneeling in a small cell. Like the guard in the previous photograph, they look directly into the camera and are enclosed within the even smaller frame of a cell, made smaller still by the cropping at the top of the photograph, which makes it appear as if the two figures were enclosed in a box so small that it would be impossible for them to stand up. The painted wall behind the guards, like the window glass in the previous shot, reflects light back at the viewer. The only visual exit in these heavily framed images is the invisible fourth wall — the situation of the photographer and finally of the viewer herself, who is dully illuminated by the light reflecting from the claustrophobic back walls of the photographs.

The strategy in both photographs of tightly framing the figures of the guards so that what is enclosed and central is their gaze looking back at the viewer could be said to enclose the viewer as well, to demand that the viewer encounter these human agents of the Third Reich's "Final Solution," and to test the viewer's own response to the fact that the guards are wounded themselves. Again, Miller provides a narrative frame that surrounds these heavily visually framed images: "Their condition is terrible, but they are still alive and not as badly off as their new captors had been when beaten, as at least they have been well fed and had never been beaten before" (*Lee Miller's War* 165). However, to look at the photographs at all, the viewer cannot look askance but must somehow make sense of the eye-to-eye encounter with these men as both agents and objects of violence and make crucial distinctions among different kinds of wartime violence. The viewer must consolidate a possibly oscillating ethical position; she must make sense of her contradictory impulses of identification, distancing, and revulsion when participating in this visual encounter.

Faced with and attempting to represent the visual evidence of the results of fascism, Miller completely eschews any trace of surrealist mimicry, of the invasion of bodies by space, that has helped her earlier photographs to hold "in view," by a series of visual contradictions, the central fact of war's damage to the human body. In abandoning the visual strategies of surrealism, Miller accomplishes a far more radical and politicized undermining of the unified seeing subject than surrealism ever could. Positioned within the frame of these images from the camps, the *Vogue* viewer is called upon by these photographs to both look and look away, simultaneously to gaze most intently and to seek a route of visual escape or relief, to look the enemy full in the face and to discount him as a full human subject, to believe the visual evidence that the photographer provides and to discount it if it is unaccompanied by a supporting or framing narrative.

Double Exposures: The Interiors of Fascism

The dynamics of war correspondence, the complex and exceedingly difficult interplay of identity and difference for the female observer of war, take a final strange turn in Miller's last report from the front, which describes her visit to Munich immediately following the defeat of Germany. What Miller photographs and describes in this report are the domestic spaces formerly occupied by Adolf Hitler and by Eva Braun. The enormous visual, political, and subjective tensions evoked by the photographs from the liberated camps are once again raised here, but now within domestic spaces used as metonymies of fascism itself. The last front of fas-

cist ideology and of the European war is, for Miller and her viewers, the
space of the domestic — space most readily known by *Vogue* readers as
the very site of the female subject as constructed by perception of the
image/commodity.

Miller's report includes a detailed catalogue, an extremely close reading of the objects in Hitler's and Braun's houses. She describes Hitler's book-
case, sculpture, and bedroom:

> In the main entrance hall were cupboards holding crystal and china, linen
> and silver, all swastika'd and initialled A.H. There was a rubber plant and
> a black plaster eagle with folded wings. His bedroom was hung with chintz
> and the bed was upholstered in the same material. The bed table had a
> push-button gadget, which had Maid, Valet, and Guard marked, and there
> was a large cream-colored safe in the corner. (*Lee Miller's War* 191–92)

Miller is even more exhaustive in her description of Braun's house:

> Part of the china was modern peasant and part was white porcelain dotted
> with pale blue flowers. The furniture and decorations were strictly depart-
> ment store like everything in the Nazi regime. . . . Eva's bed was uphol-
> stered in self-striped ice-blue satin. The linen was initialled E.B., and
> the nearly bare cupboards were equipped with chintz-covered hangers
> and padded hat stands . . . A carton of envelopes of soapless hairwash for
> blonds, a few belts, a tweed beret, and a douche bag. . . . The long mir-
> rored dressing table had . . . tweezers, Elizabeth Arden lipstick refills
> (marked Milan), a half bottle of Arden skin tonic, little funnels and spat-
> ulas for transferring beauty products. . . . Her bathroom was supernormal,
> except for two medicine chests . . . Evipan, eyewash, sleeping pills and
> nose sprays. A variety of bronchial cure-alls — gland medicines and vita-
> mins. The neighboring girls said Eva was always taking something for
> some sort of pain, especially girl's troubles. (*Lee Miller's War* 198)

Miller underscores the "normalcy" (and in Braun's house the "super-
normalcy") of these two domestic spaces, the fact that they look like anyone's house: "there were no signs that anyone more pretentious than mer-
chants or retired clergy lived there. . . . It looked like any other building. . . .

Superficially, almost anyone with a medium income and no heirlooms could have been the proprietor of this flat" (*Lee Miller's War* 191).

Like the visual fact that the beaten S.S. guards wear civilian clothes and at first appear to be objects rather than agents of violence, these verbal representations of the domestic spaces at the very center of fascist rule are not immediately identifiable as inalterably Other: these spaces and objects look like ours. Miller's detailed catalogue of these interiors is more than just an acknowledgment of the banality of evil. Her close reading of fascism's domestic spaces indicts not only fascist politics and ideology but also the far more widespread specular structures central to the construction of gendered subjectivity in Western philosophical discourse and in texts like *Vogue*. Her report constitutes a deadly serious play on the items that make up the visual and material field of the image/commodity. The scrutiny of almost every possible surface and interior space and the naming of the familiar name brands function as an enormous and grotesque parody of the pages of *Vogue* itself and of the irresolvable tensions of the position of Miller's own correspondence, set among *Vogue's* extensive advertisements.[14] It is as if the absent figures of Hitler and Braun, represented metonymically only by their domestic surroundings, have been completely absorbed into those surroundings: a political parody of the process of mimicry. The detailed verbal close-up reads as if Miller were using these items to expose the very interiors of the body of the fascist regime itself—a body surrounded by an environment not at all unlike the one inscribed in *Vogue's* advertisements and features.[15]

As if to underline this gesture of exposure, and to gesture as well towards a career spent on both sides of the camera, Miller uses her own body to construct a difficult and complex subject-object correspondence while touring Hitler's and Braun's homes. One of the photographs taken during this tour, shot by Miller's friend, the *Life* photographer David Scherman, is of Miller taking a bath in Hitler's bathtub in his Munich apartment on the day that his suicide was announced (plate 21). Miller's head, face, and shoulders are visible above the edge of the tub between a portrait of Hitler that is resting on the left rear edge of the tub and against the back wall and the statue of a female nude on a table at the right of the tub. Miller is scrubbing her back with a washcloth and looking off to the left. A pair of large and muddy combat boots rest on the bath mat and floor immediately in front of the bathtub. The photograph is a conscious, deliberate act of iconographic outrage, a bizarre juxtaposition of protected domestic space, physical and visual exposure, and military invasion. The photograph functions much in the same way as does Miller's statement in this report, "I took a nap on Eva's bed" (*Lee Miller's War* 199). Miller is reversing the fascist invasion and control of vision, sexuality, and identity, the destroyed bodies and spaces of the war, by invading with her own body at its most defenseless (in the bath, in bed, naked, asleep) these private spaces of the Third Reich. The visually evident defenselessness of her own body also, of course, underlines the defeat of the Reich, its vulnerability, the fact that it has been invaded by a "*femme soldat*" (*Lee Miller's War* 65) out of her uniform. One might also argue that the photograph chillingly restages the liberation of the tiled gas chambers of the camps that Miller had recently been photographing. What interests and disturbs me most in this image is Miller's exposure of her own body to the visible domestic traces and metonymic interiors of fascism, interiors that finally lead by visual association back to the gas chambers of the concentration camps.

After Dachau and Buchenwald, after the extremity of its vision (the disbelief it engendered in its first viewers at how the human body could look and what that appearance meant), the report from Munich seems to mark the only place Miller's representations of the war can finally go. Her dispatch is not only a report on the end of the Third Reich but also a report on the impossibility of the *Vogue* reader's innocent or apolitical identification with the image/commodity. The piece parodies the central cultural work of women's magazines using a detailed description of the personal belongings of Hitler and Braun as well as the photographer's own body, which acts as the wrench thrown into the image/commodity machine as it exposes the very interiors of the fascist state.

Conclusion

Like the fashion and surrealist milieus in which she worked and whose visual conventions she adopted, subverted, and abandoned, Miller's work was deeply concerned with the relationship of gendered bodies to space. As a photojournalist, Miller was able to politicize that relationship through her experiments with the specular subject-object relations that fashion, war propaganda, and surrealism worked to engender. Miller's tools for such an experiment were the ones she learned to use in her schooling in the surrealist movement and in the fashion industry: the formal pictorial elements of distancing, framing, fragmenting, and juxtaposition; visual metaphors of mimicry; and responses to historically specific situations of the wartime female spectator as consumer. Miller's photographs inscribed a female seeing subject constituted by enormous tensions of identity and difference, a war correspondence that truly attempted to construct its viewers as pro-Allies and anti-fascist and simultaneously to involve them in an active acknowledgment and knowledge of the physical costs of fascism and the war. That this chapter begins and ends with a photograph of Miller herself underlines what is for me a crucial aspect of her work, learned among the surrealists and in the fashion industry and central to her construction of the wartime observer: the presence of the female body at its most vulnerable, in a self-exposure that is also an exposure to and of the dangers of the specular in a belligerent culture.

Plate 1. Women at bomb shelter, 1940. Photo by Lee Miller. © Lee Miller Archives.

Plate 2.▲ "One of the Thousand YMCA Girls in France," ca. 1918. Poster by Neysa McMein. Courtesy of the Museum of the City of New York.

Plate 3.▶ "Stage Women's War Relief," ca. 1917. Poster by James Montgomery Flagg. Courtesy of Susan Meyer.

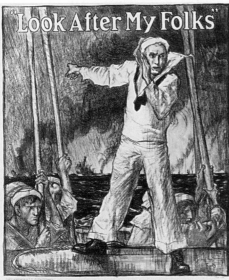

Plate 4.▲ "Help Your Country Stop This," ca. 1917. Poster by Frank Brangwyn. Courtesy of the Museum of the City of New York.

Plate 5.◀ "Look After My Folks," ca. 1917. Poster by Frank Brangwyn. Courtesy of George Dembo.

Plate 6. Edith Wharton at the French front, 1915.
Courtesy of Charles Scribner's Sons.

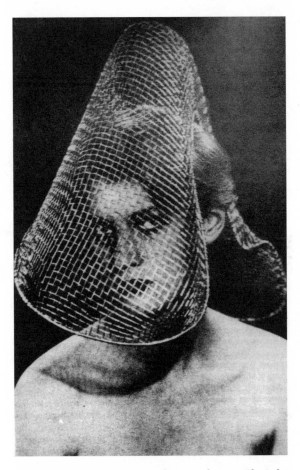

Plate 7. Lee Miller wearing sabre guard, 1930. Photo by
Man Ray. © 1997 Artists Rights Society (ARS), New York / ADAGP /
Man Ray Trust, Paris.

Plate 8. Nude with a wire mesh sabre guard, 1930. Photo by Lee Miller.
© Lee Miller Archives.

Plate 9. Lee Miller's torso, ca. 1930. Photo by Man Ray. © 1997 Artists
Rights Society (ARS), New York / ADAGP / Man Ray Trust, Paris.

Plate 10. Lee Miller at a window, ca. 1930. Photo by Man Ray. © 1997 Artists Rights Society (ARS), New York / ADAGP / Man Ray Trust, Paris.

Plate 11. Paquin's navy-blue woolen dress, Place de la Concorde, 1944. Photo by Lee Miller. © Lee Miller Archives.

Plate 12.▶ Bruyère's quilted windbreaker, Place Vendôme, 1944. Photo by Lee Miller. © Lee Miller Archives.

Plate 13.▼ Models relaxing before a fashion show, 1944. Photo by Lee Miller. © Lee Miller Archives.

Plate 14. U.S. servicewomen at a fashion show, 1944. Photo by Lee Miller. © Lee Miller Archives.

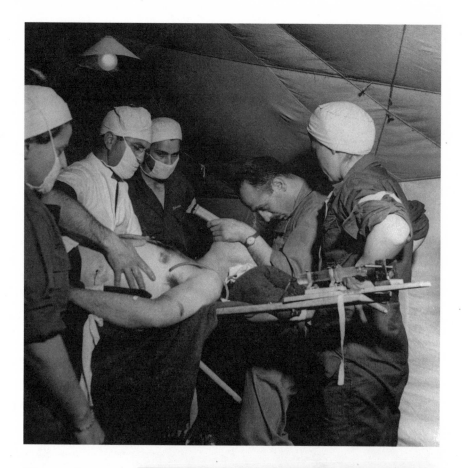

Plate 15.▲ Surgeon using bronchoscope, 1944. Photo by Lee Miller. © Lee Miller Archives.

Plate 16.▶ Burn case, 1944. Photo by Lee Miller. © Lee Miller Archives.

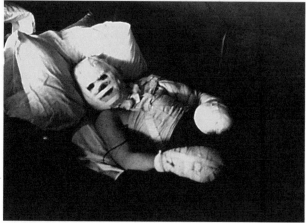

Plate 17.◀ Corpses at Buchenwald, 1945. Photo by Lee Miller. © Lee Miller Archives.

Plate 18.▼ U.S. medics, Dachau, 1945. Photo by Lee Miller. © Lee Miller Archives.

Plate 19.▶ Prison guard, Buchenwald, 1945. Photo by Lee Miller. © Lee Miller Archives.

Plate 20.▼ Prison guards, Buchenwald, 1945. Photo by Lee Miller. © Lee Miller Archives.

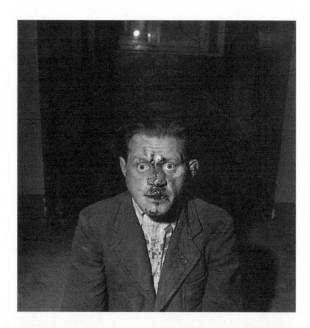

Plate 21. Lee Miller in Hitler's bathtub, Munich, 1945. Photo by David Scherman.
© Lee Miller Archives.

Plate 22. Gertrude Stein and soldiers on Hitler's terrace, Berchtesgaden, 1945.
Courtesy of the Yale Collection of American Literature, Beinecke Rare Book and Manuscript Library, Yale University.

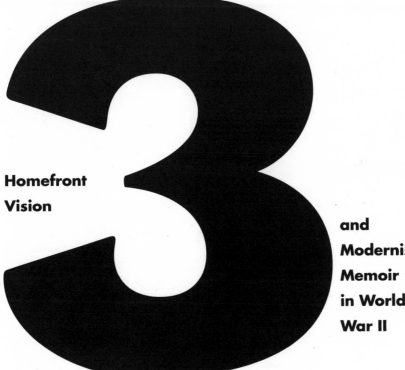

Homefront
Vision

3

and
Modernist
Memoir
in World
War II

5

Visual Disturbances in an Expanded Field: H.D. and the Blitz

For human beings collectively to orchestrate their visual experience together it is required that each submit his or her
retinal experience to the socially agreed description(s) of an
intelligible world. Vision is socialized, and thereafter, devia-
tion can be measured and named variously, as hallucination,
misrecognition, or "visual disturbance."
— NORMAN BRYSON, "The Gaze in the Expanded Field"

I do not see the picture. We are concerned with the border.
— H.D., *Within the Walls*

SIGNIFICANT PART OF H.D.'S WORLD WAR II–ERA
autobiographical prose represents the female gaze as a means of under-
standing "war, its cause and effects"[1] and as a way of constructing the female subject in a belligerent culture. Focusing on sections of "Writing on
the Wall" (composed 1944 and published in *Tribute to Freud*); *The Gift*
(composed 1941–43); and *Within the Walls* (composed 1940–41),[2] this
chapter will explore how H.D. offers her readers an expanded understanding of what constitutes seeing (and) war through her sustained attention
to the female gaze and to the relations between wartime visuality and the
specular structures of the patriarchal family.[3] In these works, war is in part
represented through the intersection of two distinct gazes or trajectories
of vision: the gaze of violence itself (military and otherwise) directed at
the body of the female observer and the observer's gaze at a hallucina-

tory image or preternaturally vivid dream-image.[4] These images, which lie outside the boundaries of shared, socialized visuality, are part of H.D.'s project of inscribing what might be called an "expanded field" of war-time vision.[5] This chapter will discuss what models of female subjectivity, both individual and collective, arise at the crossing of these gazes and how those models might function as sites of resistance to wartime visuality and violence.

The two gazes that are central to H.D.'s representation of war and its female seeing subject are clearly articulated together in a passage from "Writing on the Wall," composed in autumn 1944, several months after the January–March "little Blitz" on London and the June and July "buzz-bombing" by pilotless V-1 bombers (Calder 555–60). In this passage, H.D. describes the "light pictures" she had seen appear on the wall of a hotel bedroom during a trip to the Greek Island Corfu with her lover Bryher in 1920. Several of the images or pictures are overtly related to war: the "head and shoulders . . . of a soldier or airman" (*Tribute to Freud* 45) and a "series of tent-like triangles" that "were not so much the symbolic tents of the past battle fields . . . but tents or shelters to be set up in another future contest. The picture now seemed to be something to do with another war" (*Tribute to Freud* 55–56).

Perhaps even more important than the war-related images that H.D. sees is how she describes her own gaze at these images:

My facial muscles seem stiff with the effort and I may become frozen like one of those enemies of Athene, the goddess of wisdom, to whom Perseus showed the Gorgon head. Am I looking at the Gorgon head, a suspect, an enemy to be dealt with? Or am I myself Perseus, the hero who is fighting for Truth and Wisdom? But Perseus could find the way about with winged sandals and the cloak of invisibility. Moreover, he himself could wield the ugly weapon of the Gorgon's severed head. . . . He was himself to manipulate his weapon, this ugly severed head of the enemy of Wisdom and Beauty by looking at it in the polished metal of his shield. Even he . . . would be turned to stone, frozen if he regarded too closely and without shield to protect him, in its new quality of looking glass or reflector, the ugly Head or Source of evil. So I, though I did not make this parallel at

the time, still wondered. But even as I wondered, I kept the steady concentrated gaze at the wall before me. (*Tribute to Freud* 52–53)

While none of the separate images that H.D. sees on the wall are inherently threatening, the whole set of images is understood as a possible
representation of the "source of evil," of "another war." The gaze of the
female subject meets, through a visual disturbance or hallucination, the
menacing gaze of war itself, embodied in the ancient trope of the Gorgon's
head. The scene asks its readers to consider the shifting and contradictory
relations of the female observer to specularity and its dangers. Perseus is
invisible, bearing a mirror-shield to protect him, and can manipulate as a
weapon the image of the Gorgon. By contrast, the seeing "I" is exposed and
visible to the menacing Gaze of violence. Without the mirror-shield, the
reflecting surface or optical device that protects the hero, she is unable
to manipulate as a weapon the image she sees. For the female observer in
this passage, to stand outside of the specular protection offered by Perseus's
mirror is to risk becoming "frozen" by the gaze of violence itself—yet it
is a risk that the seeing "I" deliberately, consciously runs. This hallucination seems to constitute a slip out of the circuit that conflates visuality and
military violence, eluding or rejecting the specular surfaces of Western
culture's heroic legends; yet in doing so, it exposes the female subject to
the immobilizing threats of specularity. As we will see later in the chapter,
this contradictory relation to the dangers of a specular "freezing" is a recurring element in her prose of this period, suggesting her textual commitment to exposing herself to and making visible what is most threatening in
visuality.

Another important element of this hallucination is that through a kind
of collaboration with her lover Bryher, H.D. finds that she can control her
act of seeing:

"There have been pictures here. . . . I can break away from them now, if
I want—it's just a matter of concentrating—what do you think? Shall I
stop? Shall I go on?" Bryher says without hesitation, "Go on." . . . I knew
that this experience, this writing-on-the-wall before me, could not be
shared with . . . any one except the girl who stood so bravely there beside

me. . . . perhaps in some sense, we were "seeing" it together, for without her, admittedly, I could not have gone on. (*Tribute to Freud* 47–49)

The collaborative nature of this visual disturbance hints at the kind of collective visuality and visual threat that H.D. explores further in *The Gift* and *Within the Walls*.

Before turning to a reading of these texts, I would like briefly to discuss how H.D.'s wartime trajectories of vision might be understood within two contexts: first, developments in early twentieth-century weaponry and its creation of a civilian seeing subject of total war and second, theories concerning the menacing "gaze of the Other" as articulated by both Jean-Paul Sartre and Jacques Lacan. Paul Virilio observes that the civilian subject is especially marked by vision: "with the advent of strategic bombing everything is now brought home to the cities, and it is no longer just the few but a whole mass of spectator-survivors who are the surviving spectators of combat" (66). This civilian spectator-survivor under bombardment is also an object under a truly and physically menacing gaze that conflates weapon and eye:

> alongside the "war machine," there has always existed an ocular (and later optical and electro-optical) "watching machine" capable of providing soldiers, and particularly commanders, with a visual perspective on the military action under way. . . . one and the same function has been indefinitely repeated, the eye's function being the function of a weapon. (Virilio 3)

Virilio further notes that the spectator-survivors of war who are literally under the gaze of weaponry do not actually "see" the war in any direct, unmediated sense. Describing a military-optical process already underway in World War II, Virilio claims that "war and its technologies have gradually eliminated theatrical pictorial effects in processing the battle image. . . . the world disappears in war, and war as a phenomenon disappears from the eyes of the world" (66). The very nature of the weapons aimed at London during the blitz establishes H.D. and her fellow Londoners as "spectator-survivors" of a bombardment and as objects under a lethal and highly mediated military gaze.

A version of this threatening gaze is most famously modeled in Sartre's parable of the watcher in the park in *Being and Nothingness*. There, Sartre imagines his solitary self as the Cartesian seeing subject who is at the "unchallenged center of the visual field" (Bryson, "The Gaze" 88)—until the entrance into the park of another person who "decenters" and displaces him from his privileged subject position (Sartre 254–302; Bryson, "The Gaze" 88–89). For Lacan, this decentering of the observer is set in motion not so much by the intrusion of another person on the field of vision as by an irremediable state of "being seen" by a disembodied, unlocalizable "gaze," mediated by a network or "screen" of social signification that is beyond the control of the individual subject (Bryson, "The Gaze" 91, 94; Lacan 74).[6]

Critics often describe this gaze of the Other in military or otherwise violent terms, linking the very construction of the seeing subject with conflict and confrontation.[7] Bryson maintains that this notion of the "terrorizing" gaze is a limited one, as it tends to regard "terror as intrinsic to sight" and to exclude analyses of historical change, cultural specificity, and shifting power relations such as those of gender and race, which in fact can render sight terroristic ("The Gaze" 105).[8] In response to theories of the terrorizing gaze, Bryson suggests that visuality can be construed "as something built cooperatively, over time" for which members of a culture are "ethically accountable" ("The Gaze" 107).[9]

It is among these kinds of conflicting gazes and visual possibilities that H.D. places the female observer in her World War II–era prose. For H.D., the Blitz—the literal, menacing gaze of the German bombardment of London—is one extreme manifestation of a terrorizing gaze that she also encounters in the violent, specular visuality of the patriarchal family. In response to this menacing gaze, her work inscribes the female observer's hallucination or "visual disturbance," which represents or "give[s] body to" (Lacan 84) the terrorizing gaze in visible form. The female observer of war and other forms of violence in H.D.'s work is often represented as occupying the border or boundary of the visual field constructed by the violent gaze, gesturing toward or indexing "something" that would contain or surround that gaze within an expanded field of vision.[10] While it is certainly important to place H.D.'s concern with mystical "vision" within the long history of female (wartime) prophecy,[11] I would also suggest that H.D.'s privileging of "visual disturbances" in her Blitz-era prose might be read as a form of discursive civil disobedience by which she represents the female seeing subject as one exposed to what is most terroristic in visuality — both within the family and within a scene of military engagement — in order to explore the possibilities and limits of a collective, "ethically accountable" wartime visuality.[12]

While the Gorgon's-head passage discussed above identifies the menacing gaze of the Gorgon with the gaze of military action, *The Gift* charts the female subject's childhood entrance into, and later adult survival in and resistance to, the terroristic visual realms associated not only with military violence but also with the specular visual relations of the family.[13] H.D. plots the conflicting gazes or looks in *The Gift* through a series of juxtaposed family parables and personal memories. The entire first chapter, "Dark Room,"[14] shows the development (literally and figuratively, as the photography metaphor of the title suggests) of Hilda's vision, that is, vision as learned, socialized, and gendered. With its descriptions of Hilda's learning to see through a variety of optical frames — telescope, microscope, and proscenium arch — the chapter establishes *The Gift* as a memoir of the female subject's first encounters with technologies of vision and violence and of that subject's first forays into an expanded visual field.

This chapter links learned, developing, gendered vision to violence, particularly through images of the wounded or dead bodies of women. The opening sentences immediately associate or juxtapose Hilda's family history, family photographs, and the witnessing of a girl's death:

> There was a girl who was burnt to death at the seminary, as they called the old school where our grandfather was principal. . . . the girl who was burnt to death, was burnt to death in a crinoline. The Christmas tree was lighted . . . and the girl's ruffles or ribbons caught fire and she was in a great hoop.
>
> The other girls stand round. There is Mama . . . and Aunt Laura . . . and Aunt Agnes in her long frock, who in the daguerreotypes and old photographs looked like the young mother of the two little girls. . . .
>
> But the girl in the crinoline wasn't a relative, she was just one

of the many girls at the seminary when Papalie was there and she screamed and Papalie rushed to her and Papalie wrapped a rug around her, but she is shrieking and they can not tear off her clothes because of the hoop. (1–2)

The parable of the burning girl is immediately entangled with family history, inherited images, and the construction of gender. The description of the girl caught in the hoop of fire, literally trapped in the clothing that helps to construct her as female, is reminiscent of Bryson's description of the Lacanian theory of the Gaze, in which "the vocabulary is one of capture, annexation, death" ("The Gaze" 108). While the first image of this childhood memoir is so clearly menacing for the female subject, it is not the entry into visuality itself that is "intrinsically disastrous" ("The Gaze" 107), as Bryson claims it is for Lacan; it is rather the actual damage, caused by uncontrollable forces, witnessed by and done to young girls, that renders vision terroristic. "The other girls stand round" presumably to witness the death of this girl, but the girls are also seen as they are in pictures. Their passive act of witnessing this death is inextricable from their status as objects of sight.[15]

If the female gaze in these early pages of *The Gift* suggests a passive spectator of uncontrollable disaster, another parable in this first chapter represents a potentially more active and harmful female spectator of war. This parable, in which Hilda's father is the object of his mother's mistaken (and emotionally damaging) sight, is important to the text's representations of gendered vision and war:

papa had been a soldier. . . . He and his brother Alvin had gone off, and Alvin had died of typhoid fever. Papa had typhoid, too. He said his mother cried when she saw him come back; she said, "Oh, I thought it was Alvin, coming back." Papa never told us much about himself except that his mother had been disappointed when she found it was Charles and not Alvin who had come back from the Civil War. (6)

Hilda's father's reading of his mother's tears suggests that the weeping mother is at best hostile and callous about the life of her soldier-son. The son's implicit interpretation of the mother's gaze and her reaction to what she sees recalls in a slightly different form Schweik's examination of a long tradition in Western war poetry of a vicious female spectator who employs "a rhetoric peculiarly feminine, ignorant and instigatory, spoken and published only from safe parapets and behind enclosed walls" (96).[16]

Immediately after the first chapter's narrative of a mother's mistaken look at her soldier-son, the text turns to the gaze of that son, now an adult, a father, and an astronomer, whose profession is related to the exclusion of his young daughter from the act of seeing:

> Papa went out to look at the stars at night. He measured them or measured something, we didn't know quite what. . . . when Papa took us into his little domed house . . . and we asked to look into his telescope, he said that we would see nothing; you could not see what he was looking at, or looking for, in the daytime. . . . When we kept on asking him to let us see, he did let us see, but it was as he had told us; there was only a white glare and nothing to be seen and it hurt your eyes. It would be too late to go over there at night, he said, and anyhow at night he was busy. (7)

If optical devices like the telescope tend to maintain the strict binary of subject-object positions,[17] the young girl in this scene is barred from a subject position: she can see nothing, and the "subject-effect" (Bryson, "The Gaze" 100) created by a viewed object at the other end of the telescope is negated. Hilda's father is, like Sartre's solitary watcher, master of all he surveys and its sole, controlling surveyor. Like Irigaray's model of the male philosopher of specular thought, he is in a "closed chamber . . . the matrix of speculation in which he had cloistered himself in order to consider everything clearly" (192). The father's telescope in the "little domed house" further recalls Irigarayan notions of specularity, as the young girl encounters under his tutelage, in his philosopher's "matrix of speculation," the "nothing to be seen" that confronts the female subject when she looks into the specular mirror of patriarchal visuality.

The father, the philosopher and speculator, the owner of the mirror in which the female sees (her own) "nothing," is further associated in this text with violence and dead women in Hilda's family history. Immediately after the description of the father's telescope, the narrator says,

I can not say that a story called *Bluebeard* . . . actually linked up in thought—how could it?—with our kind father. There was a man called *Bluebeard*, and he murdered his wives. How was it that Edith and Alice and the Lady . . . all belonged to Papa and were there in the graveyard? No, of course, I did not actually put this two-and-two together. (7)

The juxtaposition of the parables of the paternal grandmother's mistaken vision, the father's telescope, and the legend of Bluebeard closely link gendered vision and gendered violence in *The Gift*'s first few pages.

The text makes connections between the paternal specular gaze and specifically military violence in a description of two closely associated dream images. The first revolves around a drawing in one of Hilda's childhood books that illustrates and defines what a "nightmare" is and explores the female subject's early encounters with images of violence and death, images in which the female body is simultaneously an explicit target of menace and an object of the specular gaze. I quote at considerable length in order to underline the way the text works through juxtaposition:

There was another book with a picture; Mama cut it out. Because Mama cut it out, it was there always. . . .

The picture was a girl lying on her back, she was asleep, she might be dead but no, Ida said she was asleep. . . . the picture was called *Nightmare*. . . .

. . . it was a witch on a broomstick, but the book was science, they said it was to explain real things. Then the witch was real; in Grimm it was a fairy tale but a witch in a book called *Simple Science* that someone gave us must be real because Ida said that was what science was. Papa and Papalie were working at real things called science; the old witch was riding straight at the girl who was asleep. It was a dream; Ida said, "Nightmare is a dream. That picture is to explain what a nightmare is."

. . . "It was only a picture, I cut it out," [Mama] said; you could see how she had cut it, the picture was gone.

"What is a nightmare?"

"It's a name for a bad dream." . . .

"Is it a night horse?"

. . . A night mare is a mare in the night. . . . it is something terrible with hooves rushing out to trample you to death. . . . He goes out in the night.

"What does he do there?" . . .

"I've told you and told you and *told* you, he goes out to look at the stars." (50–52)

This passage describes the early gendering of sight and its connection to menace or threat. The female subject who looks at the picture is subject to two visual controls: the mother's excision of the picture and the exclusionary frame of the father's specular telescope. The girl in the excised picture is in an extremely passive position under the targeting gaze of the witch "riding straight at her." The nightmare-image and its threat to the female subject under the gaze is associated with the father's "scientific" nocturnal gaze at "nothing." Hilda's questions about the "reality" of the image suggest that for the female subject, the gendered visuality that identifies the "real" with the father's scientific discourse can indeed be menacing. That the mother's attempt to cut out the threatening image renders it more clearly and permanently "there" again suggests that the female seer-observer is committed to attempting to incorporate or contain the embodied, imagined gaze of violence in an expanded visual field.

In the following chapter, the narrator recounts a nightmare that she apparently has at the time of the writing of the narrative, during a bombing raid. The narrator intercuts discussion of the dream with more childhood memories concerning the nightmare image from *Simple Science*:

This is the python. Can one look into the jaws of the python and live?
. . . The python took shape, his wings whirred overhead, he dropped his sulphur and his fire on us.

"Why did you cut out that picture from this book, Mama?" . . .

"Oh — I — I thought you would forget." . . .

Look at its face if you dare, it is meant to drive you crazy. It is meant to drive you mad so that you fall down in a fit like someone in the Bible and see a light from heaven. (58–60)

These two passages represent several key moments in the construction of the female look at and under a menacing Gaze. They conflate the father's specular, exclusionary look, the image of the female body exposed to danger or death, and the extreme menace of the "fire and sulphur" of the blitz. The python is the very face of military destruction. Like the Gorgon-head in "Writing on the Wall," it is the intensely menacing gaze of the militaristic Other that looks at and offers itself to the look of the female subject, even though to "look at its face" would be to court exactly the kind of wartime "nerve disorders" that H.D.'s work is so bent on understanding and avoiding, a madness understood in terms of vision or an excess of vision.[18] The narrator does, however, "look at its face," just as she looks at the Gorgon's head of her hallucination in spite of her acknowledgment of its specular dangers. Again, the female gaze in the expanded field must attempt to incorporate rather than excise the threatening image or the terroristic gaze.

The expanded field of vision mapped in *The Gift* also makes possible a nonterroristic gaze within or at the borders of patriarchal visuality. Hilda's grandfather's microscope, an alternative to the father's telescope, is one model of such a possibility. The grandfather, like the father, is first described in "Dark Room" as participating in visual realms inaccessible to Hilda:[19]

> our grandfather . . . had a microscope and studied things and drew pictures of branches of moss that you could not see with your eyes. He put them on a glass slide or pressed a drop of water from a bottle . . . between two glass slides. That (in time, it was explained) was fresh-water algae, a sort of moss, invisible (for the most part) to the naked eye. The apple of my eye. He was the naked eye, was the apple of God's eye. He was a minister, he read things out of the Bible, he said, *I am the light of the world* when the doors opened at the far end of the church and the trays of lighted beeswax candles were brought into the church by the Sisters. (9–10)

The grandfather is part of a closed circuit of scientific and divine vision, the "naked eye" under the eye of God; speaking for and as God, he claims to make sight itself possible. However, the first important difference between the father's and the grandfather's optical frames is that of inclusion and exclusion for the female subject: "You could see what Papalie showed you. You could not see what it was that Papa went out to look at" (50). In a remarkable passage in the first chapter, the text juxtaposes Hilda's learning to see through the grandfather's microscope with her first attempt at spelling. During a game of anagrams, the mother praises Hilda's brother Gilbert for spelling "d-a-g," while Hilda's aunt observes "'d-a-g doesn't spell anything that I know of; Sister would know an *a* from an *o* if you don't, Gibbie'" (10). The narrator then says, "and it might even be perceived that miraculously, a round shape in black, on the yellow square of cardboard, was somehow alone and staring at me, by Aunt Jennie's elbow" (10). As in the scenes containing the Gorgon's head and the nightmare of the python, the gaze directed at the female subject is an embodied image, albeit far more abstract than the Gorgon or the python, and far from threatening. We see a mutual gaze between the developing female subject and the letter; both participate in the spelling out of linguistic and visual meaning.[20]

This sudden image of the letter O is immediately associated through juxtaposition with Hilda's seeing through the grandfather's microscope:

> It was a game, it was . . . a way of spelling words, in fact it was a *spell*. The cuckoo clock would not strike; it could not, because the world had stopped. It was not frozen in time, it was like one of Papalie's water-drops that he had brought down from the mountains. . . . It was a drop of living and eternal life, perfected there; it was living, complete. . . .
>
> When Papalie lifted us, one by one in turn, to kneel on the chair by his worktable, we saw it was true what he said, we saw that where there is nothing, there is something. (10–11)

The letter O staring back at the female subject who overtly recognizes that "where there is nothing, there is something" suggests how part of *The Gift*'s work is to create a female seeing subject that begins to circumvent the "freezing" specularity of the menacing gaze and the exclusive subject-object positions reified by patriarchal optics. The nothing-to-be-seen of female sexuality in specular thought is suddenly visible; the letter O, the hoop, the sign of female subjection to danger and/as visuality suddenly looks back, a sign of her knowledge of difference (the nothing to be seen) and, simultaneously, of the questioning of sexual difference (where there is nothing, there is something).[21] Moreover, the living, complete "something"—the visual plenitude from which the female seeing subject had been excluded by the father's telescope — that is seen through the grandfather's microscope and the associated mutual gaze with the letter O emerging from the edge of the visual field are made visible within the confines or enclosures of patriarchal visuality.

Like the other women whose works are examined in this book, H.D. often relies on a verbal index to gesture toward what resists representation in normal visuality. For H.D., this often manifests itself as "something" indexed at the edge of a scene of violence and as "something" resistant to the specularization of the female body and violence to that body. One example is in H.D.'s 1928 review in *Close Up* of Carl Dreyer's film, *The Passion and Death of a Saint*. H.D. criticizes the film's representation of violence in scenes depicting the torture of Joan of Arc: "I do mind standing aside and watching and watching *and* watching and being able to do nothing" (132). Like *A Stricken Field*, this review protests the use of vision as torture, of the enforced seeing of violence as a kind of violence itself.[22] H.D. seeks another, redemptive visual order, not representable in any overtly visual way, at and beyond the boundaries of the scene:

> There is another side to all this, there is another series of valuations that can not perhaps be hinted at consistently in this particular presentation of this one kicked little puppy of a Jeanne. . . . Isn't it just that? . . . I do not mean to say that there could have been any outside sort of beatific screen craft of heavenly vision. I don't mean that. But Jeanne kicked almost . . . to death, still had her indomitable vision. I mean Jeanne d'Arc talked openly with angels and in this square on square of Danish protestant interior, this trial room, this torture room, this cell, there was no hint of angels. The angels were there all the time. . . . Such psychic manifestation I need hardly say, need be in no way indicated by any outside innovation of cross lights or of superimposed shadows. It is something in something, something behind something. (132–33)

Like the "something" that makes *A Stricken Field*'s American journalists look at Rita but that resists definition and specularization, the "something" that H.D. seeks in the film can only be gestured toward from the edge or border of the scene of patriarchal violence.

Another meditation on "something" at the borders of visuality occurs midway through *The Gift* as the narrator describes a boat trip during which Hilda, her brother, and her father see a large group of water lilies:

> They were not at first there, but as the boat turned round and shoved against the bulrushes and then the bulrushes got thinner and you could see through them . . . you saw what was there, you knew that something was reminded of something. That something remembered something. That something came true in a perspective and a dimension . . . that was final. (72)

The expanded, ecstatic field of vision, discovered as a result of the father's invitation to "[c]ome and see" (70) is a totalizing, "final" one, superseding or containing all perspectives, to the point where the "something" indexed here includes not only the object of vision but the subject as well. Like the "something" viewed through the microscope, the vision of the water lilies suggests that the expanded field of vision can be mapped onto and can surround the plane of patriarchal visuality.[23]

A similar indexing of a larger field beyond the border of normal visuality takes place in the opening paragraph of "The Dream":

> The dream escaping consciousness is perceived. In one vivid moment, it may be held, circled in a ring of complete understanding. Then it leaps the rope of the tightening lasso, and we are almost glad to see it has gone. The dream is gone now, it is running wild in the pastures of the mind's *hinterland.* (605)

While in her prewar film review, the "something" almost glimpsed at the edge of the visual plane is an unambiguously redemptive one; this "something" in the hinterland of visuality is, presumably, the image of the menacing, military gaze itself—the nightmare image from *Simple Science,* which is described later in the chapter and is associated with the blitz-related dream of the python, discussed above. Again, H.D. emphasizes how the potentially redemptive image she is seeking to represent during the Blitz is often the violent signifier itself, briefly "circled in a ring of complete understanding" and then set in an expanded visual field that gestures beyond the parameters of "the socially agreed descriptions of an intelligible world," beyond the confines of terroristic vision, the hoop of fire that immobilizes and threatens the female observer of violence.[24]

The opening paragraphs of "The Dream" constitute a primer for the construction of such an expanded visual field, as H.D. directs her readers toward an imagined landscape in which the boundary or border around intelligible visuality is transgressed but not destroyed:

> The dream, the memory, the unexpected related memories must be allowed to sway backward and forward, as if the sheet or screen upon which they are projected, blows and is rippled in the wind of whatever emotion or idea is entering a door, left open. The wind blows through the door, from outside, through long, long corridors of personal memory, of biological and race-memory. Shut the door and you have a neat flat picture. Leave all the doors open and you are almost out-of-doors, almost within the un-walled province of the fourth-dimensional. This is creation in the truer sense, in *the wind bloweth where it listeth* way, in the way the snow falls, in the way a branch of mock-orange blossom runs askew out of its frame. (606)

The crucial word in this passage is "almost." H.D. takes pains to emphasize the continued presence of the confining structures located within and supporting the expanded parameters of her revised visuality: the screen, the frame, the in-doors, the walled province of the house. H.D.'s screen, reminiscent of the "screen of signs consisting of all the multiple discourses on vision built into the social arena" that Lacan insists is "inserted between the retina and the world" (Bryson, "The Gaze" 91–92),[25] is disturbed or "rippled" in H.D.'s expanded field, but it remains intact. The frame is what makes the "running askew" possible; the walls, as H.D. claims in her wartime poem *Trilogy*, "do not fall" (*Collected Poems* 507).[26]

H.D.'s *Within the Walls*, a collection of brief autobiographical and dream narratives composed during the first blitz on London in 1940 and 1941, locates the expanded field and the female wartime observer within the downed walls of the bombed city, "almost out-of-doors," but not quite. The partially destroyed walls scattered across this text's landscape provide

H.D. with another means of mapping the expanded, collectively constructed visual field that will contain the menacing gaze/image of wartime weaponry and visuality.

In the first and title sketch, the opened walls clearly signal the dangers of wounding and the absolute necessity to survival of maintaining the integrity of the body's boundaries. Having survived a night of bombing, the narrator announces, "January 14, 1941 is like a window miraculously unbroken in a house holding firm above the earthquake. . . . We have a secret. We are alive. . . . we are within the walls of our bodies, for the time being. This is a notable experience" (2).

The walls in this sketch also are the city walls, which indicate and isolate the community under bombardment: "Those without the walls, *extra muros*, even here in England, have already separated themselves . . . from this particular crowd, that has endured for such a long time, at such intensity, unprepared . . . to meet the eventuality of death. . . . there is the difference, there are those *extra muros* and those *intra muros*" (1). Here, the blitz creates its own containment, clearly marking the ground-zero of danger on which the inhuman gaze of the unpiloted buzz bombs is trained. However, in another dream narrative in the collection, a house damaged by bombardment but still standing, its interior exposed and visible, suggests that the space opened by the menacing gaze of weaponry is simultaneously open to the incursion of redemptive elements from the "hinterland" of visuality:

> The side of a room, my own room, seemed to have slid away, but this was not unpleasant. It was suggested no doubt, by the houses we see, with rooms open to the street like stage-rooms, some are neatly sliced off with furniture still standing. . . .
>
> This open-to-the-street room is dim, but now snow swirls and drifts . . . into the room. . . . it fills the room as air made visible.
>
> Through the rifts there are stars. . . .
>
> It is a dream of peace and hope. It seems to indicate that though our houses and our minds have been sliced open by the attacks of the enemy overhead, that, overhead is as well the great drift of stars, and those stars found entrance into the shattered house of life. (25)

Once again H.D. positions the female seer-observer of total war at the boundary of the target area under the menacing gaze. This gaze is contained or encircled by an expanded visual field in which it occupies only one small and decentered part. And once again, H.D. makes clear that such a placement is critical to her project of "fight[ing] in the open . . . war, its cause and effects" and the "war-terror" (*Tribute to Freud* 94) that had haunted her, and European culture, for decades.

The broken walls that mark the open borders of H.D.'s wartime visual field constitute a potentially liberating landscape for the female wartime observer. By contrast, to leave certain walls intact and certain visual images unexposed is to suffer greater dangers:

> a chance glimpse of illustrations in the Book of Martyrs or some picture from our illustrated Gustav Dore bible or the Ancient Mariner which we spread open, before we could read, on our grandmother's carpet, seared deeply, awakened one's mind to the actual reality of death.
>
> What was not fully understood . . . was tactfully slurred over;
>
> "What is this, in the Ancient Mariner?" "O, it's some spirits, angels." "And this skeleton?" They could not say, "that is Death." They say, "O, it's just a picture in a book." The picture remains after later reading is forgotten. . . . What is it that I am afraid of? Well, before the night is over I may be caught in a blaze of falling timbers, be burnt (out of the Book of Martyrs) to death. But we must not think of being burnt to death. The Book of Martyrs disappeared, along with the pictures in the Ancient Mariner.
>
> It is the unseen, the unrealized, the deeply immured image that is the most dangerous. The present shock may crack the wall of an old immured shock. (10–12)

This passage's connection between the childhood "immured image" of death and the immediate dangers of the blitz is mediated by a dialogue between Hilda and "them," adult members of her family, who, in order to protect the child from the implications of the image, underline its status as "just a picture," denying its representational power. Such a denial, like the mother's attempt to cut out the illustration of the nightmare in *The Gift* is, H.D. claims, at least as dangerous as her exposure to the gaze of weaponry.

However, it is these very same adults in Hilda's extended family who are her earliest mentors in understanding the nature of representation in an expanded field of vision. In the "Dark Room," a chapter of *The Gift*, the narrator describes how, during a local theatrical production of *Uncle Tom's Cabin*, several "university boys" in the balcony laugh during the performance. These viewers are "extra muros" to the young narrator, who delineates a community of seeing that privileges several kinds of visual perception:

> Lots of people do not know the things we know and that Uncle Tom was seeing a vision, like something in the Bible, when he saw Little Eva . . . standing against the curtain that had wings painted on it. . . . only maybe the university boys . . . didn't know how to look at pictures or to see things in themselves and then to see them as if they were a picture. (17)

The community of vision, the "we" of Hilda's family, offers her instruction in seeing, involving an oscillating look that takes seriously both the visual sign and its hallucinatory referent.

As I suggested in discussing H.D.'s description of her "steady concentrated gaze" at the Gorgon's head of military visuality, her wartime writing suggests the possibility that the expanded field of vision that contains and decenters the gaze of patriarchal and military violence might be collectively constructed. *Within the Walls* offers another parable of collaborative, and specifically female, visuality in one of its dream narratives:

> Now, my mother is showing me a piece of tapestry, embroidery. It is apparently my own. I am not satisfied with it, but "see," she says, "the pattern is not broken." I am sure the stitching is slipshod and badly done but she says, "no, look, there is the one line running through it all." There is a somewhat vague tapestry edge to the center picture. I do not see the picture. We are concerned with the border. It is a wave pattern, the curves meet and run along symmetrically the whole length. Then the wave pattern seems to dissolve or resolve into fleur-de-lys. . . . "Look," my mother says, "the pattern runs right to the end," as if she wanted to assure me that

the pattern of my life was right, that the thread would not be cut abruptly, that I was weaving toward an established end. (5)

This "concern with the border" of the visual field, indexed by her mother's insistent "see" and "look, there is . . . ," is precisely the concern that H.D. seeks to elicit in her readers. The contradictory pattern, simultaneously unbroken, dissolving, and resolving at the margins of the central "picture" that it surrounds, recalls the broken walls of the blitzed building open to the drift of stars, the redemptive "something" at the edge of the scene of violence, the menacing dream in the hinterland of the visual field held momentarily in a totalizing "ring of complete understanding": the various sites where H.D. maps the expanded field of wartime vision in her attempt to contain and decenter the menacing gaze of patriarchal and military violence.

6

Occupation and Observer: Gertrude Stein in Vichy France

URING THE VICHY REGIME AND THE NAZI OCCUPATION of France, Gertrude Stein was engaged in producing an unusual form of propaganda and an unusual model of the female civilian observer under the visual and discursive limits of military occupation. Unlike the World War I propaganda discussed in earlier chapters and the official propaganda produced by the Vichy government, Stein's did not attempt (however unsuccessfully) to construct a unified, militarized subject who would support particular wartime policies nor a central, privileged position from which to view war. Stein's wartime writing instead actively undermined interpretation of visual and verbal evidence in order to elicit American sympathies not so much for the entire Vichy regime (about which she reveals very little knowledge in her writing and which she almost never names) as for two public figures in particular: Philippe Pétain and Gertrude Stein. In effect, Stein disarmed her American readers, seeking to defer judgment about particular visual experiences of the civilian observer of the occupation, about France and its head of state, about political and historical events, and about herself until after the war's end.

This strategy can be understood as one response to the difficult, dangerous — one might say untenable — political situation Stein was in, that of a foreign Jewish lesbian living in Vichy France. Stein's work suggests how the German occupation and Pétain's National Revolution — with its extremely conservative social agenda, its surveillance of the civilian population, and its persecution and eventual deportation of political and ethnic minorities — raised continual questions about the interpretation of visual and other evidence, particularly concerning individual identities and political loyalties and made answering those questions a menacing proposition. Who is a collaborator? Who is a member of the Resistance? Who will be denounced by whom? How accurate are the reports of German atrocities? When will the war end and who will win it? During the occupation, Stein tried to keep these questions afloat in her writing, but she actively deferred the answers, continually undermining her own assertions about, and avoiding explicit interpretation of, visual experience and historical events. Stein arguably engaged in such a practice during her entire career,[1] but during the Vichy period, the practice took on very significant political color.

Modeling the interpretive uncertainty and confusion surrounding visual experience that characterized life in France during this period, Stein attempted to promote in her readers a kind of *attentisme* — the political attitude of "wait and see" common among French citizens during the occupation[2] — in order to suspend judgment of the leader of the Vichy government and of her own decision to remain a resident of France during the war. With the success of the Resistance and of the Allied landings, Stein was able to interpret visual data in a more coherent, consistent political scheme. As I hope to make clear at the end of this chapter, the end of the war signaled the end of deferred political and visual interpretation for Stein and her readers. Moreover, the image of Stein herself became a visual sign of political certainty through the liberation-era photographs of her published in the American press.

What follows is a reading of Stein's 1942 "Introduction to the Speeches of Maréchal Pétain," her autobiographical narrative, *Wars I Have Seen* (composed in 1943–44 and published in 1945), and her 1945 *Life* magazine article, "Off We All Went to See Germany." Tracing the historical trajectory from occupation to liberation, this chapter explores Stein's struggles with Pétainist propaganda, the representation and interpretation of wartime visual evidence, and the status of the foreign female observer during military occupation.

Stein biographers and critics have often disagreed, and have had to try to reconcile what appears to be contradictory evidence, about Stein's political leanings during World War II. Most biographical sources acknowledge that Stein and her partner Alice B. Toklas received special protection from their local prefect as a result of their long-standing friendship with Bernard Fäy, who became the head of the Bibliothèque Nationale during the Vichy regime.[3] Linda Wagner-Martin, examining what she calls Stein's "double life" during the occupation (246), refers to Stein's "Introduction to the Speeches of Maréchal Pétain" as "apparent propaganda for Vichy" (247) but uses Toklas's and other postwar memoirs to suggest that Stein and Toklas "were relieved" when Fäy was unable to visit them (246) and to suggest that they had visits from members of the Resistance during the war, who provided them with freshly baked cakes and with "sheets of gelatin used for making false identification papers" (239)[4] and who were "'collecting and transmitting information to them'" (251). Marianne DeKoven writes that Stein "allied herself politically, if at all, with an anarchic but generally right-wing American 'rugged individualism'" but also claims that Stein's 1940 essay, "The Winner Loses: A Portrait of Occupied France," "is a tribute to the *maquisard* Resistance near her home in Belley" (*Rich and Strange* 200).[5] Shari Benstock characterizes Stein's politics as "complex" and writes that "Stein was not openly a Nazi sympathizer" but that her "anti-Semitism was a mark of her own self-hatred as a Jew" that "allowed her to turn a blind eye to the fate of other Jews, and . . . blinded her to the gravity of her own situation during the Second World War" ("Paris Lesbianism" 338). Benstock concludes that Stein's politics are perhaps most marked by a certain political ignorance: "it remains unclear whether she ever understood what was at stake in this war, what had led to it, or what her own position was in it" (342). Most recently, Wanda Van Dusen accepts as a given Stein's "political conservatism" (70) and suggests that the "Introduction" to Pétain's speeches—Stein's most explicit statement of support for Pétain—can be read as "redemptive fetishistic ritual that denies the existence of racism in the so-called free zone . . . administered by Pétain" (71).

It is vital for any reader of Stein's occupation-era writing to bear in mind that French public opinion about the Vichy government and its policies was rife with conflict and underwent enormous changes during the four years of the occupation. Robert Paxton writes that "[b]y 1944 the universe had so completely turned on its axis that the main strategic assumptions of 1940—short war, British defeat, danger of revolution, imminent peace—seemed nonsense" (45). However, there is some disagreement among historians as to when such a turn in events and opinion became obvious to the majority of French citizens. Most historians maintain that the Vichy government suffered its definitive loss of support in late 1942, following the Allied invasion of North Africa, when German troops occupied all of France, and not just the northern half of the country, or in early 1943, when Prime Minister Pierre Laval instituted the extremely unpopular program of le Service du Travail Obligatoire (STO), which drafted young French citizens for forced labor in Germany.[6] Paxton identifies spring 1943 as the moment of "'total disenchantment' of public opinion with the government" (327), although John Sweets argues that many areas of France were hostile to Vichy's social policies, propaganda, and surveillance well before that date (98). H. R. Kedward and Roger Austin suggest that before the definitive downturn in Vichy's status in late 1942–early 1943, ambivalence and ambiguity marked a great deal of writing all across the political spectrum (5–10).[7]

In tracing the changing fortunes of the Vichy government, many historians point out that it is important "to distinguish adequately between attitudes toward Pétain himself and popular opinion regarding the government and its programs" (Sweets 146). While Vichy's socially conservative and politically collaborationist policies grew more unpopular during the last two years of the war, Pétain himself during much of the Vichy period enjoyed such a degree of popular acclaim that many contemporary observers and historians have described it in terms of religion (Kedward, *Resistance in Vichy France* 12; Flanner 41).[8] Kedward notes that during the first two years of the occupation even the anticollaborationist press displayed ambivalence about, rather than explicit criticism of, Pétain.[9]

I provide this brief overview of some of the questions and ambiguities facing historians of Vichy France because I believe that this context, largely neglected in Stein criticism, is crucial for a reading of Stein's occupation-era writing. This writing is remarkable in that it inscribes and participates in the intensely conflicting and changing discourses of popular middle-class French public opinion that surrounded Stein in the department of the Ain from 1940 to 1944.[10] Her reluctance to interpret visual experience; her admiration for and doubts about Pétain; her representation of multiple French points of view about Vichy, Germany, and the Allies; and her seeming obsession with food,[11] all reflect to some degree the culture and politics of the French countryside that she and Toklas inhabited. Stein's writing about Pétain and about her perceptions (visual and otherwise) of occupied France changed quite significantly as the war went on, reflecting the shifting perceptions and loyalties of the great majority of French citizens. The complexity that Benstock rightly sees in Stein's wartime politics is in part so complex because it modifies significantly over time and constructs Stein and her readers as political and seeing subjects in very different ways at different points in the war and, in *Wars I Have Seen*, at different points within a single text. Marjorie Perloff claims that "Stein's urge is to minimize temporal distinctions, to present us with a spatial figure, a synchronicity, analogous to the flat or planar landscape of a Cézanne or Picasso" (97). I hope to show how the "temporal distinctions" and political fluctuations of the Vichy period are central to Stein's construction of the observer of the occupation, particularly in *Wars I Have Seen*.

Before turning to *Wars I Have Seen*, the work that best embodies these "temporal distinctions" and that most explicitly seeks to suspend, manipulate, and direct readerly interpretation of visual experience during the occupation, I would like to examine Stein's most overtly propagandistic work, her unpublished "Introduction" to her own translations of Pétain's *Paroles aux Français: Messages et Ecrits* (1941), written for an American audience whose country had just entered the war.[12] To postwar readers, Stein's timing and her sense of her audience may seem anything but propitious; it is difficult for us to imagine that in January 1942 Stein could assume sympathy on the part of her American readers toward the head of a government collaborating with an American enemy.[13] Her own publisher, Bennet Cerf of Random House, called the piece "disgusting" (qtd. in Van Dusen 70) and never published it. However, it is important to remember that the

United States and France maintained diplomatic relations throughout the war (Paxton 129) and that at the time when Stein was writing the "Introduction," the extent of Pétain's active collaboration with the Third Reich was just beginning to become clear to and be discussed in the clandestine Resistance press.[14]

At the time Stein was writing the "Introduction" (late 1941), Pétain's popularity was still strong in France, although historical evidence suggests that ambivalence and outright criticism were on the rise.[15] One of the salient characteristics of Stein's "Introduction" is that it inscribes the political and perceptual tumult of the Vichy era, fragmenting the models of collective and individual subjectivity that propaganda more often attempts to render coherent. Moreover, it models the suspension of interpretative certainty that Stein explores at great length — and in direct relation to visual experience — in *Wars I Have Seen.*

In the "Introduction," Stein immediately announces her text's intended audience (Americans) and its propagandistic agenda (to elicit sympathy for and understanding of Pétain and the French nation that supports him by creating a sense of parallel interests and experiences between France and America now that the United States has entered the war):

I want to present to my compatriots the words that Marechal Petain has spoken directly to the French people, Marechal Petain who in the last war saved France by a great victory and in this war has saved them throughout their great defeat.

I am well aware that until just now it would have been quite impossible to interest my fellow countrymen in these words which tell so convincing and so moving a story.

We in the United States until just now have been apoiled [spoiled] children. Since the civil war until to-day, when the action of Japan has made us realize the misery the grief and the terror of war all this time because we have tender hearts we have always felt for others and helped them all we could but we did not understand defeat enough to sympathise with the French people and with their Marechal Petain, who like George Washington, and he is very like George Washington because he too is first in war first in peace and first in the hearts of his countrymen, who like George Washington has given them courage in their darkest moment held them together through their times of desperation and has always told them the truth and in telling them the truth has made them realize that the truth would set them free. (93)

As in much propagandistic writing, this piece opens with an assumption of a shared "we," "compatriots" with a common history and common emotional responses to political events.[16] Stein seems to compound the gesture toward a unified political subject through the apparent conflation of Pétain's and her own words: "these words which tell so convincing and so moving a story" might refer to the words of Pétain's speeches or her own "Introduction" to the speeches. However, the unified "we" of this opening paragraph changes and fragments in the next paragraph, as Stein shifts to an authorial identity with the French and then indicates how that national entity is riven with differing ideas about Pétain: "We have not all of us and I too have been of that number over here in France always had faith in the Marechal but in the end we have all come to have faith, and now I will tell a little more what he has done and how he has done it and why I want everybody in America to realise it" (93). As is the case with the later *Wars I Have Seen*, Stein here emphasizes the problem of uncertainty and of fragmentation and the lack of unified opinion. The subject "We have not all of us" indicates the breaking up of the unified pronoun of propaganda, and even when the paragraph finally arrives at certainty ("in the end we have all come to have faith"), the writing itself undermines that faith by continually representing doubts and disunity.

One example of this is the representation of the controversy around Pétain's age:

Everybody worried about his age was he too old to last out . . . [was] he too old to go on saving them, he undoubtedly had saved them, was he too old to resist what there would be to resist. In short was he too old.

He was old but gradually it was decided that he was not too old. . . . they realised that being as old as he was and not having a family, he had no future, he had only the future of France, and as French people mistrust people who have a future they could put their trust in the Marechal because he being as old as he was and without a family had only France's future and so they pretty well all of them did trust him. Longevity is always respected in France and this longevity of the Marechal was a very special thing and so they did trust him and when he told them anything he told them the truth and very often he did not tell them anything. (94)

While one might argue that Stein's propagandistic agenda is served by modeling for her readers the shift from disagreement to consensus,[17] she continually undermines that consensus by introducing new elements of discord. Once Stein arrives at that final statement of unified French opinion, she undermines it by making an ambivalent statement about Pétain's communicativeness and honesty with Vichy subjects. Stein is here tapping into one of the common themes of Pétainist literature: Pétain's "sparing and considered use of language" (Proud 63). However, as a propagandist setting out to introduce Pétain's "truthful" speeches to an American audience (who would not have had the same kind of exposure to Pétainist literature), Stein subverts her text's own explicit intentions by indicating that Pétain often was not forthcoming with his audience.

In her attempt to elicit American sympathies for France, Stein refuses to indicate French support for an Allied victory. In fact, she takes pains to describe significant French ambivalence about the Allied effort against Germany:

Then came the time when the French people gradually came to feel what they did feel, what they always do feel that they do not at all think alike all of them about everything. As a Frenchman explained it to me it is not only that they do not think alike with their neighbor but they do not think alike within themselves. As he said, you take any French one, that one French one has quite logically perhaps four points of view. Supposing he has a son a prisoner, well he wants the war over as quickly as possible so that his son will come home, so he wants the Germans to win as that would finish the quickest, at the same time he is a business man and he wants business to go on, and that would only happen if the Germans were defeated and England won, then he wants the Marechal and as the English are opposed to him they would insist on bringing back into France all the people who helped to ruin France so they do not want England to win and then there is Russia, and that is ever more complicating. You see said this Frenchman no Frenchman can feel simply about this thing. (94)

This passage accomplishes several contradictory things. First, Stein's refusal to model for her readers a united France and her presentation of a "French one" who at least sometimes would prefer a German victory in the war demonstrates the apparently self-subverting method of her propagandistic writing. However, by modeling the multiple points of view of French citizens, Stein is inscribing a political subject marked by ambivalence — a state that, I would argue, the text aims to promote in its American readers as Stein seeks not their judgment but the suspension of judgment.

This passage does, though, suggest ways that Stein assumes some implicit shared political beliefs on the part of her readers, herself, and the unnamed Frenchman. "Wanting the Marechal" is to be understood as a given, a fact much in the way having a son as a prisoner or being a businessman is a fact, requiring no explanation or justification. Missing from this presentation of the multiple points of view in French popular opinion at this point in the war is the one that did not support Pétain.[18] The passage assumes that readers will agree that the English "would insist on bringing back into France all the people who helped to ruin France" and that France had indeed been "ruined."[19] Stein's deliberate refusal to identify "the people" indicates an assumption of agreement and understanding from her readers, much in the same way she assumes that her readers will be able to fill in the clause that should follow "and then there is Russia" with some shared response. Stein appears to assume, in fact, that her American readers already share the political stance of the majority of French citizens at this point in the war, a stance that centers on "faith in the person of Marshal Pétain," suspicion of Communist influences, disenchantment with the Third Republic and the Popular Front, and the view that Vichy seemed to be the only legal alternative for government (Paxton 236–37). Van Dusen writes of this passage that the figure of the Maréchal "is cast as subsuming and thus resolving the opposing 'points of view.' . . . the invisible face of a diverse population [is] obscured by the unifying state mask of the Maréchal" (81). A question remains, however, as to the effect of such an assumption of shared political stances: do the implicit political positions tend to include readers in a shared point of view or alienate them from the self-contradicting French subject that Stein is constructing? My sense is that Stein leaves her American readers suspended among the many French "points of view," several of which are not fully articulated.

The "Introduction" is in fact so troubled by its inability or refusal to make consistent assertions that it often describes no action at all on the part of the Maréchal but rather only the welter of disagreement he occasions, rendering somehow laudable Pétain's lack of action or explanation for his actions as well as Stein's own refusal to describe that action:

> And then gradually the Marechal either did what any one and every one thought he ought to do or he did not, and whether he did or whether he did not and nobody really knew there was one thing that was certain and that was that like Benjamin Franklin he never defecnded [defended] himself, he never explained himself, and in short his character did not need any defense. (95)

This passage appears to defeat the announced discursive agenda of the text as a whole by refusing to make any kind of assertion about its ostensible subject. What did Pétain do? Why did he do it? What did the French think about it? None of these questions is answered, countering Stein's promise of the first few paragraphs to tell "what he has done and how he has done it and why I want everybody in America to realise it" with an almost explicit refusal to offer any information whatsoever. This sort of red herring is a recurring feature in Stein's work, particularly in the relationship between title and text. Perloff notes of *Paris France* that while the book conveys very little information about "French history or geography, . . . it creates a verbal space we come to recognize as, so to speak, *Stein France*" (98–99). The space created by Stein's representations of Pétain might indeed be understood as a region of "*Stein France*," but it is also populated and fragmented by the contesting discourses of French citizens in Vichy.

In her representations of Pétain, Stein is drawing on a discursive constant of Vichy France, what Janet Flanner in her 1944 profile of Pétain referred to as "*la mystique autour de Pétain . . .* a strange, esoteric state religion" (41). In a study of Vichy propaganda in children's literature, Judith

Proud demonstrates how many visual and narrative texts of the period "endow their hero [Pétain] with mythological status and near-sainthood" (58). According to Kedward, the rightist intellectual Charles Maurras had "equated Pétain with truth, about which there could be no opinion" ("Foreword" vi). Pétain's World War I military career occupies a significant part of government discourse in Vichy France, as it does in Stein's writing.[20]

It is, however, important to observe not only the similarities but the differences between Stein's language and that of official Pétainist propaganda. Stein asserts Pétain's unique status and its basis in his World War I– era heroics, and she echoes the popular understanding of the Armistice as a way of protecting France from greater German incursions. However, unlike much of the propaganda to which she was exposed during the Vichy period, Stein refrains from asserting the unity of France and its empire but instead seems to question that unity by her insistence on representing divergent points of view. Even as Stein holds forth the centrality of the individual leader as grounds for political hope, she does so in the midst of repeated doubts about Pétain's ability to protect the French from German occupation policies:

> We used to stand on the country-roads and discuss, this time the Marechal had given in, and we almost were sure that he had given in. Gradually they began to tell that when he was asked who was going to win the English or the Germans, he did not answer and when he was pressed he touched his breast and answered Moi I Moi.
>
>   I cannot tell you how many times in this long difficult year we thought many of us thought that he had gone under, under one thing or under another, and we all talked and talked but no, the Miracle which is a miracle, and his defense of his armistice has been a miracle went on being a miracle, and here still is. (95)

Stein's text in fact shares patterns of ambiguity with much of nongovernment-sponsored literature published in Vichy France, which Robert Pickering describes as

> a complex . . . system of self-censorship and correction . . . favouring an atmosphere of ambivalence . . . a discourse which on one level is situ-

ated firmly in the *status quo*, in the acceptance of a dominant mode of
thinking but which on another level is constantly subverting the authority of its own message by reflection, retrospective wondering, doubts and
questioning. (261, 264)

However, while the ambiguities, doubts, and questions within Vichy-era
fiction appear to have cut against the unifying agenda of official government discourse, Stein's textual contradictions may be understood as actually furthering her text's agenda—not so much to elicit overt American
sympathies for Pétain and for herself as resident of Pétain's France but rather
to place her readers in a state of interpretive suspension. The void that this
suspension creates allows a small textual space where the figure of Stein-
in-Vichy can reside, temporarily free of readerly critique.

This space grows ever more central in Stein's longest autobiographical
work of this period, *Wars I Have Seen*. According to the dates that recur
throughout the text, *Wars I Have Seen* was composed between April 1943
and August 1944, charting Stein's perceptions of the last sixteen months of
the Vichy regime, the period following the total occupation of France that
saw massive deportations of French and foreign Jews, a precipitous decline
in popular support for the Vichy government, the consolidation and success of the armed Resistance groups, and the Allied invasion of France.
Like most of the texts discussed in this study, *Wars I Have Seen* problematizes the notion of the unified seeing subject of war and the specular promise of completely achieved wartime visual perception. In its gradual turn
from occupation to liberation, the text also turns from the deferral of interpretative certainty regarding visual and verbal evidence concerning political activity in the area surrounding Stein's village and the fragmentation
of political subjectivity to the possibility of interpretive certainty and of a
unified subject.

In *Wars I Have Seen*, Stein's representation of the fragmentation of the
political subject in France, particularly in regard to Pétain and the armistice, recurs, but with some significant differences. An early section of the
text explicitly concerned with Pétain and written in the fall of 1943, well
after the point when the Vichy government enjoyed much in the way of
popular support, contains enormous tensions, reflecting Stein's struggles
between her own continuing support for the Marshal and her observations

of the effects of the STO (the law that drafted young French citizens for forced labor in Germany) and the occupation of the entire country. On one hand, Stein represents herself as participating in the vagaries of French public opinion after the signing of the Armistice: "And then there was Petain. So many points of view about him, so very many. I had lots of them, I was almost French in having so many" (82). On the other hand, Stein separates the narrating "I" from the oscillations of French popular politics, rewriting a passage from the "Introduction" to emphasize her distance from the French position that supports German military efforts:

> After the armistice in '40 I was surprised, I can always be surprised, but I was decidedly surprised, so many of them were not sure that they did not want the Germans to win. And I said why, I do not understand. . . . why, I said why, and I said it pretty violently and pretty often. The man at the bank explained something. He said there are a great many different points of view and one single man can have quite a great number of them. . . . Any one man, said the man at the bank, could want the English to win, because as he was in business he wants business to be secure, and if the Germans win business would not be secure not for him, at the same time he has a son who is a prisoner, his only son, and he wants the Germans to win because his son would come home to him, and if the English were to win the war would be long and his son might die before he came home to him, then at that time Germany was allied to Russia and might that mean communism and then he would want the English to win, and then there is another point of view, that French love to talk about discipline, they always think their country is very disorderly as a matter of fact they are so traditional . . . they like to think there is no order and that there should be. That is Petain's point of view, that was the point of view of a crazy man at the end of the last war in 1918, who one day started to ask every body to show him their papers at the station . . . and when the man had been taken to the police court and had been asked why he had gone on like that answered, because I want to put a little order into my country. (81–82)

This version of the conflicts in French public opinion also deletes the earlier reference to "the people who ruined France," and the assumption that "wanting the Marechal" is a position that requires no explanation, thus erasing the implicit suggestion that Stein's readers and the French public share a set of political assumptions. Moreover, Stein adds a new "point of view" in which she posits Pétain's and other French citizens' desire for more "order" as an absurdity.[21] Pétain, appearing in the "Introduction" as the stable point at the center of multiple points of view, is now represented as the fallible holder of one such point of view, comparable to that of "a crazy man."

Stein also implicitly ascribes to the French, with their puzzling political stances, her own narrative habit of deferring explanation and interpretation, again distancing herself from those stances:

> Then gradually things changed the Russians became Germany's enemy, and the French were having more points of view in one man than ever. . . . The most astonishing people . . . said they would if they were younger go and fight the Russians, what I said with the Germans well not exactly, against the English well not exactly, well what then I said, and they said well what, and that conversation ended. (82)

Stein's strategy of deferral creates a great deal of discord in these passages concerned with Pétain. Several times Stein seems on the verge of disclosing her own thoughts about Pétain ("This is what happened to me about him" [82]; "But to tell about Petain and all the things one could I could think about him" [83]), only to interrupt and defer the fulfillment of this expectation by describing local farmers' responses to the German-Russian conflict, Parisian jokes about Hitler and Napoleon, the relative merits of sugar and honey (a distinction made necessary by wartime rationing), and most important, her neighbor's unhappiness when their son is drafted into the STO. It becomes clear through a report of a dialogue between Stein and the boy's mother that he is choosing to join the "mountain boys" and to resist the STO ("and she said no, no, he will not leave, he will not leave" [84]). After representing these various voices of French disagreement and discontent, Stein finally returns to the subject of Pétain and the history of her own thoughts concerning him. Her statements veer from critique ("I did not like his way of saying I Philippe Petain, that bothered me" [87]) to unqualified support: "Petain was right to stay in France and he was right to make the armistice and little by little I understood it. I always thought he was right to make the armistice" (87–88). Even when Stein makes her strongest statement of support for Pétain, the juxtaposition of this statement with so many notes of distancing and disagreement once again fractures the unified subjectivity of wartime propaganda, suspending herself and her readers in the interpretive void.

While the "Introduction" and several passages of *Wars I Have Seen* represent the fragmentation and contradictions of collective political positions in France, the greater part of *Wars I Have Seen* is concerned with the construction of the individual political observer in the shifting visual field of the war and the occupation. Stein expressed the notion of the decentered wartime seeing subject in a passage from her 1938 essay "Picasso," where World War I is understood primarily in terms of changes in visuality, in the historical conditions of seeing:

> Really the composition of this war, 1914–1918, was not the composition of all previous wars, the composition was not a composition in which there was one man in the centre surrounded by a lot of other men but a composition that had neither a beginning nor an end, a composition of which one corner was as important as another corner, in fact the composition of cubism. (37–38)

For Stein, the seeing subject of World War I is radically disembodied. It is not identified as either combatant or civilian, male or female. The gendered subject and object of vision, the "man in the centre surrounded by a lot of other men," that constitutes the "composition of all previous wars" disappears from the "cubist" wartime landscape. Encountering Stein's claim in this same essay that "[a]t present another composition is commencing, each generation has its composition, people do not change from one generation to another generation but the composition that surrounds them changes" (38), readers of Stein's later works are left with the question: what is the "composition" created by the occupation and liberation of France? What kind of visual field does Stein offer her American readers? How is the seeing subject situated on that field?

In struggling with representing the "composition" of the occupation and the position of the seeing subject in that composition, Stein suggests early in *Wars I Have Seen* that there is no privileged position from which to perceive a war completely, including that of male combatants:

There is one very funny thing about wars as a child sees it, although there are so many killed there being so many dead is not very real at all. . . . However near a war is it is always not very near. Even when it is here. It is very funny that but it is true. Perhaps if one were a boy it would be different but I do not think so. I think even when men are in a war actually in a war it is not very near, it is here but it is not very near. That is the way it seems to me from all I can hear and from all I can see. (9)

In contrast to the "cubist" composition of multiple, equally important, disembodied viewpoints, the war Stein describes here provides multiple observers with no viewpoint at all from which to "really" perceive the war. The new composition that emerges is comprised of negative assertion ("not very real," "not very near") and of continual distancing from the object of perception, "even when it is here." However, this passage does reassert the presence of embodied observers (a child, I, a boy, men in a war), even as those observers are all to a certain extent removed from the wartime visual field. In its attempt to suspend readerly engagement with visual evidence, Wars I Have Seen frequently offers such a nowhere from which the observer might view the events of the occupation.

Wars I Have Seen actually models the narrowing of the visual field during the occupation in the shift from its first fifty pages, which consist primarily of autobiographical and theoretical musings about "war" as an abstract quality, to the remainder of the text, which offers a representation of Stein and her neighbors in the villages of Belley and Culoz from April 1943 to August 1944. The book's opening pages seek to establish guidelines for understanding the connections between representations of war and early subject formation. This first section of Wars I Have Seen continually problematizes the three substantive words of the title, "wars," "I," and "see," subjecting them to a kind of semantic bombardment that renders them unstable. In doing so, Stein at least partially dismantles the notion of unified, complete vision of war, refusing to provide a central perspective or privileged subject position from which to view the war. At the same time, she temporarily expands the possible interpretations that adhere to the notions of war, subjectivity and vision — an expansion that will in turn be radically diminished when the text turns to a representation of current events.

The first sentence of the text immediately calls into question the status of the "I" whose memories will constitute a significant portion of the narrative: "I do not know whether to put in the things I do not remember as well as things I do remember." By beginning the narrative with this declaration of uncertainty, Stein announces the instability of the narrative "I" and the veracity of the material that that voice offers to readers. Stein later articulated this notion of a multiple narrator in the 1946 "Transatlantic Interview." She claimed there that two kinds of writing—narration and translation—were constituted by the incorporation of "other people's words":

> other people's words are quite different from one's own and . . . they can not be the result of your internal troubles as a writer. They have a totally different sense than when they are your own words. . . . this brought me to a great deal of illumination of narrative, because most is based not about [sic] your opinions but upon someone else's. . . . the narrative in itself is not what is in your mind but what is in somebody else's. [In writing *The Autobiography of Alice B. Toklas*] I had done what I saw, what you do in translation or in a narrative. I had recreated the point of view of somebody else. (505)

Stein claimed in the interview that among her works of "narration," "I think *Paris, France* and *Wars I Have Seen* are the most successful of this. . . . in *Wars I Have Seen* and in *Paris, France*, to my feeling, I have done it more completely" (505). While Stein's 1946 comments about the centrality of "someone else's opinions" in her wartime translations and narratives might be read as her own version of the postwar apology of Vichy supporters,[22] they also ask us to consider Stein's narrative "I" as a site of instability and difference.

A similar undermining of semantic stability occurs with the word "see." Early in the text, she claims to have "seen" three wars:

> Born that way there is no reason why I should have seen so many wars. I have seen three. The Spanish-American war, the first world war and now the second world war . . . I suppose it is not so remarkable that I should have seen so many wars having seen a good many countries when I was a baby and having a feeling about countries which I suppose sooner or later since wars are make you be one of those that see them. (4)

This passage establishes several different kinds of categories or distinctions among ways of perceiving wars (seeing and remembering) and among different kinds of perceiving subjects (those who see wars and those who don't). One might infer that for Stein, seeing war is not natural or inevitable but the result of a particular kind of subject-construction and a particular kind of perceptual experience that is not linked to direct visual perception of combat; certain conditions that have nothing to with combatant-status "make you be one of those that see" wars. Even within the category of wars that she has seen, the reader might infer significant differences that undermine any stable meaning for the word "see." Did the child living in the United States, the adult in Paris delivering supplies for the American Fund for the French Wounded,[23] and the elderly resident of occupied France "see" all of these wars in the same way? The conflation of these three experiences suggests that the word "see" invites many possible interpretations, none of which Stein makes explicit.

The word "war" is subjected to a similar kind of destabilization. In the opening section of *Wars I Have Seen*, "war" is to a great extent a discursive event, linked to family narratives and to other forms of cultural representation such as theater, film, and historical narrative. The text continually conflates war with representation of war, even as it seems to be offering some distinction between "real" wars and not-real wars. Stein specifically juxtaposes her early memories and her early perceptions of "war" with her first experience of theater: "In London there was no war no war at all but the first theatre I ever saw" (6). She continues this line of association between representations of "Indians," how "war" as a discursive construct played a role in early subject formation, and how "war" is both "real" and representation:

> I do not remember that we saw Indians but I was told afterwards that we had, and now for almost a great number of years there was no war, there was history of course and there was the civil war which had been but otherwise there were no wars. Such wars as there were inside in me. . . . Of course there were Indian wars naturally there was no cinema then but if there had been, Indian wars would have been like that, although one could know people who had been in them and could see them the real Indians on the stage and there was Fenimore Cooper they were not real

wars, not as real as some English wars in history and certainly not as real
as the American civil war. A very real war. (6, 8–9)

Stein compounds the confusion of representational elements by juxtapos-
ing "war," historical narratives, fiction in general, and historical fiction in
particular: "During these years there was no war and if there was it was not
any war of mine. But of course there was history, and there were novels,
historical novels and so there was in a way war all the time" (7). Again, war
is something that exists primarily as a text; the distinction between "actual"
war and wars in novels and historical novels is blurred.[24]

Stein not only attempts to erase distinctions between war and different
types of war narrative; she also conflates narratives about wars and readers
of those narratives: "As an omnivorous reader naturally there was a great
deal of war" (9). The absence of any pronoun in the sentence (one most
expects to see "I") identifies the reader and the reading; the reading subject is subsumed in the process of reading about war, which is conflated
with war itself. And yet, even as the text conflates these categories, it also
takes pains to try and reestablish them:

And so from the time I was little all through my adolescence although I
read and read about wars, if you like history and historical novels you have
to and historical plays, but there was no really outside war at least none
that I noticed or that anybody around me noticed. (10)

In this opening section of *Wars I Have Seen*, "war" becomes inextricable from peacetime culture and perception. The title's implicit promise
of the revelation of specific, personal, privileged visual experience of "war"
is undone, as that vision becomes shared, textualized, and connected to
family, childhood memory, and to various forms of narrative and other verbal representations. Stein's early mentor William James observed that "Perception . . . differs from sensation by the consciousness of farther facts associated with the object of the sensation" (723). In Jamesian terms, Stein
might be understood as attempting to expand the perception of war in this
section of the text by associating it with "farther facts" than are usually associated with it. Like H.D., Stein appears committed to placing war in the

context of other aspects of discourse, visuality, and subjectivity, particularly childhood and family as sites of subject formation.

However, as a reading of the rest of *Wars I Have Seen* will make clear, Stein engaged in precisely the reverse strategy in her description of her and her neighbors' lives in occupied France, as she attempted to cut away the "farther facts" of the occupation, stripping the narrative of interpretation of visual experiences. Several Stein critics have remarked on her James-inspired project "to disrupt habits of attention in order to gain insight into the unseen" (Wald 238). My sense is that Stein's interruption of her readers' interpretative processes, of placing the "farther facts" of association at as great a distance as possible ("not very near," as Stein would have it), is tied to her particular wartime agenda: modeling for readers the extremely constrained visuality of the occupation in order to postpone readerly judgment of this Vichy resident and Pétain supporter.

For the most part, *Wars I Have Seen* offers its readers a series of daily events and visual experiences, primarily domestic and local, which Stein often describes but refuses to interpret for her readers. Like the "Introduction" to Pétain's speeches, it both approaches and avoids assertions of political certainty. The text enacts how the occupation itself constitutes a suspension of meaningful visual and verbal interpretation for Stein and her readers.

A good example of how Stein presents puzzling scenarios to her readers and then refuses to interpret them occurs in a passage that, according to the dates Stein frequently uses in the text, was written around November 1943, although it is unclear when the event itself might have taken place:

We had a friend whose name was Gilbert and he was gone away and his wife followed him and the little girl Christine was left behind with some neighbors, we did not know them and one day a red-headed and active young fellow asked for me and I saw him and I said what and he said I have a message to you from Gilbert, ah I said is the little girl not well, oh yes he said she is all right she is staying with us, ah yes I said, do you need anything for her, I said and he said no she was allright and he was fiddling with a matchbox and I said well and he said the message is in here and I said you had better go, and he said are you afraid of me and I said no and you had better go and dont [sic] you want the message he said and I said no you had better go and he said I will go and he had tears in his eyes and he went out and told the servant that we had not received his message and a friend said were you not curious and I said no not.

There are so many ends to stories these days so many ends that it is not like it was there is nothing to be curious about except small things, food and weather. (100)

Immediate questions arise for the reader. What is the message? Why is it in a matchbox? What is Gilbert's background, and why has he "gone away"? Why has his wife followed him? Where have they gone? Why is Stein the intended recipient of the message? [25] The questions that the passage raises are "answered" in this way: "there is nothing to be curious about except small things, food and weather." Readers are implicitly asked to suspend curiosity, modeling themselves after Stein and her proclaimed lack of curiosity ("were you not curious and I said no not").

In a slightly later passage, written in April 1944, Stein once again models her refusal to interpret visual and aural evidence:

To-night that is this evening I was taking a long walk up the mountain and of course it was bright daylight and as I was coming down far beyond any houses, Basket began to bark at a man and I called him and when I came near I saw he was not a man from around here, he had a grey suit of cloth and a cane and a stiff brimmed hat and a rain coat over his arm, and he had bright blue eyes and a large nose and was very sun burned and had the button of the legion of honor and another decoration that I could not make out and he wore a wedding ring, and Basket continued to bark he does not at the country people because he knows what they are and I said in French he is not dangerous he is only barking and he said is he a can- iche and I said yes and he said in English he is a good doggie and I said in French no he is not dangerous, and it did seem to me that he empha- sized the last e in doggie and what naturally did that make him and one is always a little nervous you never know and we went on down Basket and

I did and he went on up and after a while I looked up and he was looking down and I came home and I asked Alice Toklas what she thought about it but naturally there was nothing to think about it, there never is, no there never is. (173)

This puzzling little parable of identity and appearance, like the story of the man with the matchbox, seems designed to raise questions for the American reader — or assumes an impossible shared knowledge. What naturally *did* that make him? (French? German? A member of the maquis? A member of the Milice, the French militia committed to carrying out deportations and combating the Resistance?)[26] Why is one always a little nervous? Is Stein nervous about being found out as a speaker of English?[27] Again, like the story of the matchbox, this one seems to have political implications that are not evident. Stein pays careful attention to the visual details of the man's accessories (his ring, clothing, facial features, and decorations) and his vocal inflections, but she refuses to indicate the significance of this evidence. She suggests the process of her own interpretation but does not tell her readers what it is. The story ends with the assertion that "there was nothing to think about it," explicitly claiming that the story has no possible interpretation and that "there never is" one. Again, the occupation seems to suspend the act of interpretation.

Yet another passage that presents the reader with uninterpreted visual evidence and then almost explicitly asks readers to defer interpretation is one in which Stein describes a day trip to Aix-les-Bains, also during April 1944:

we do from time to time go to Chambery for the day or Aix-les-Bains for the day and we did yesterday, only when you do you come back having seen something and it is change but in a way just saddening. When we got to the station there were about 30 young fellows standing each with their suit case and an overcoat and one does not see that so often, they are Italians who have been taken to go to work or French who have been taken to work in Germany, but they usually go in ordinary passenger trains but these were going into freight cars and that usually is only done with soldiers. . . . and so it did look rather sad, and they told us they were young

men and girls that had been rounded up in Annecy and were being taken
well somewhere, did they have any reason for being taken, well probably
and where were they being taken nobody ever does know. (172–73)

The passage demonstrates once again Stein's refusal to provide herself or
her readers with an interpretation — or even an accurate description — of
visual evidence. The passage shows the changing process of her identifying the group, whose nationality and gender seem unclear. The passage's
visual confusion (French or Italian? Fellows only or young men and girls?)
is matched by Stein's evident struggle to understand and excuse Vichy deportation policies, although it is unclear to the postwar reader whether this
particular group of young people is being "deported" as part of the STO
or as part of the deportations of Jews and political enemies of Vichy.[28]

As the text progresses, it continues to accumulate pieces of incomprehensible visual "evidence" that elude interpretation. Another example,
from May 1944:

Passing by the railroad tracks there are of course a great many freight cars
because the trains go through here all day long and the freight cars seem
to come that is they have the name of the town where they belong printed
on them, the other day I saw a whole train with Breslau and Koenigsberg
and Luxembourg and all the Polish and East Prussian towns that are in
these days in the news, it did seem strange to see these freight cars here in
this country so far away so awfully far away, and how do they get here and
why, well this I do not know nor does anybody else here, but here they are,
war is funny because here they are. War is funny. (180)

These freight cars are a piece of visual evidence that seem to gesture toward a narrative, but Stein instead models how interpretations, attaching
narratives of cause and effect, are postponed in the constricted field of
occupation-era visuality: "this I do not know nor does anybody else here."
Postwar readers will of course wonder if these freight cars were involved in
the deportation of Jews, another layer of anxiety and distress that this text
creates for its audience. Again we see how Stein's scenarios cut closer to the
"sensation" end of the perceptual spectrum as the "associations" or "farther
facts" of "how" and "why" are suspended.

In Van Dusen's unfinished essay, Michael Davidson has written a conclusion that suggests "[i]n her late works about occupied France, Stein seems to violate her early prescriptions about seeing as intensely as possible. Now in order to see clearly she must avert her gaze, avoid seeing an occupying force as operatives of fascism" (87). Alternatively, I would suggest that in *Wars I Have Seen*, Stein's gaze is not so much averted as restricted to attempting to register visual "sensations" without articulating the associations these sensations carry. The freight cars, the German troops, the group of young deportees on the platform, the man on the mountain, and the matchbox with the unread message are present in the text as a kind of visual data, but the interpretation of the significance of these data is deflected.

One of the first instances in *Wars I Have Seen* of Stein's offering her readers some "farther facts" associated with a visual experience occurs in a passage written in May 1944:

> Today when I was crossing the railway track I saw a long train filled with soldiers and each freight car had a flag that at a distance looked like the tricolor of France, and I had a funny feeling, naturally, but when I came near I saw that instead of red white and blue, it was black white and red, and I did not understand because the German troops never have flags, it is funny, I just realised it now, but all the German soldiers that we have seen and gracious goodness we have seen an awful lot of them on foot in cars and these last years on the railroad, but never never at any time did any of them have a flag, it is rather strange that and strange that I never was conscious of it before until to-day the fifteenth of May nineteen forty-four, when I did see a flag hanging out of each freight car filled with soldiers, the train paused and I asked the woman at the crossing what that flag was, oh she said those were Italians and that flag is the one they use for the soldiers that fight for Hitler, so that was the flag of the new fascist republic. At least they have a flag, even if the German soldiers have none.
>
> I suppose these Italian soldiers are being brought into France to fight, but well they never not any Italian soldiers that we have seen and we have seen a lot of them were ever very enthusiastic about fighting even when they looked like winning and now, well it certainly is and now. (183–84)

Stein's interlocutor's answer actually provides Stein and her readers with two levels of interpretative information. The flag is "the one they use for the soldiers that fight for Hitler"; this leads to a conclusion: "so that was the flag of the new fascist republic." However, even while providing her readers with a rare instance of interpreting visual evidence without hesitation or uncertainty, Stein pulls back from any larger interpretation at the end of the passage: "and now, well it certainly is and now." While appearing to make some sort of definite assertion ("well it certainly is"), the sentence lacks a complete predicate (is what?). This refusal allows the text to remain in a kind of discursive neutrality, even as the movement toward interpretation of visual evidence suggests the progress of the war toward the German defeat.

As the possibility of an American landing in France appears more and more likely, the struggle in the text between certainty and uncertainty grows even more pronounced. However, even as late in the war as spring 1944, one of the few kinds of discourse in *Wars I Have Seen* that does allow for an assertive interpretation of visual evidence and military event is prophecy, the only discourse that allows for the play of meaning-making. Stein's concern with prophecy also repeatedly marks her earliest Occupation-era writing, "The Winner Loses," and extends well into the last months of the war:

> will they ever come well anyway I have always been quite certain that there will be no landing until Rome is taken, I have been certain of this more than a year more and more certain, certain because it is reasonable and then there is always Saint Odile, and a saint having a vision has to be reasonable and it would be reasonable to wait for the landing in northern Europe until Rome is taken and Saint Odile did say that when Rome was taken it would not be the end of this war but it would be the beginning of the end and that too is reasonable. It is very reasonable to be a prophet if you see a thing completely and reasonably and even if it is 500 years away that makes no difference being reasonable and complete and have a complete vision is all right and natural, and anybody is more or less a prophet more or less more or less, but Saint Odile is quite completely a prophet and Rome will be taken and then a week or two after there will be a landing and we are listening in American English to what everybody is expected to do. (*Wars I Have Seen* 187–88)

Like the other texts discussed in this study, *Wars I Have Seen* does finally posit an ideal of complete, assured, privileged wartime vision, but it is the mystical vision of St. Odile, the patron saint of Alsace, and whose "prophecies of evil to come from 'the Antichrist from the Danube'" were invoked by Alsatian refugees forced to leave Alsace after refusing to abandon their French citizenship (Paxton 55). Stein's repeated assertions of certainty ("I have been certain of this more than a year more and more certain, certain because it is reasonable") are buttressed only by the narratives of prophecy itself rather than by any strictly "visible" evidence.

In the days and weeks following the Normandy landings and the retreat of German troops from France, the text reveals considerable new anxiety about the shift in political power that is accompanied by a new caution and anxiety about seeing. Stein, who up until this point in the text has been very reluctant to interpret the limited visual evidence she provides her reader and whose definition of "vision" seems most solidly based on five-hundred-year-old prophecy, suddenly becomes concerned with the precise meaning of "having seen a maqui." Moreover, this anxious desire to see a maqui is accompanied by a distrust of visual evidence, a concern about the ability to distinguish between "real and false maquis" (218) that is part of a larger anxiety about the dangers inherent in the near-civil war conditions that accompanied the victory of the Resistance:

> It's a funny life all right, so far we ourselves have not seen any maquis. I went on a long walk yesterday and went over a road that had been barricaded, just trees pulled to the side of the road, all the telegraph and telephone wires down, they had not fought there but it was certainly like a battlefield, it is hard to tell who is maqui and who isnt [sic], they have an arm-band but naturally when they come home to see their people and they all do they keep it in their pocket and then there are still some firm reactionaries who are convinced that all maquis are terrorists, we have some charming neighbors who are like that and it worries me because after all people get angry and things might happen to them and we are very fond of them. (206)

This anxiety is also accompanied by some confusion in the text over the difference between a "mountain boy" and a "maquis." Kedward points out that while many of the *réfractaires* who hid in the mountain ranges of France to escape the STO later participated in the more formally organized and armed Resistance movements, many others did not take part in more militant resistance to Vichy and the occupation forces ("The Maquis and the Culture of the Outlaw" 233). The interpretative dangers of this phase of the war are increased by Stein's confusion about naming the political factions at work: "There is one thing certain now it is very bad form to mention maquis or mountain boys, you speak respectfully of the French army, in two days the word maquis no longer exists it is with great pride the French army" (*Wars I Have Seen* 209–10). Again, for Stein, anxiety about seeing is closely tied to political uncertainties and their accompanying worries: "So far we none of us have seen any maquis, not the Canadians that are supposed to be with them, but we will they all say we will. Everybody is worried and a little confused in their minds except about the Germans that they will go" (212). The desire to ensure having seen a maqui is linked to unnamed worry and confusion about political power in the transitional phase from occupation to the reestablishment of an independent French government.[29]

When Stein finally does see a member of the maquis, she is scrupulous about recording the physical details of the experience:

> Today we were over in Belley the third of August, nineteen forty-four, and I looked anxiously to see a maquis. We still have Germans here so up to now we have had no maquis. But Belley which is maquis headquarters was unfortunately empty they had gone away to fight and I only saw one at a distance in a nice khaki suit, that is shirt and trousers, with a red cord over his shoulders so we came home satisfied we had seen a maquis. (222)

It is only after the liberation of Paris, when maquis are in charge of policing and supplying the region in which Stein lived that the text loses its traces of ambivalence about the maquis (who they are, what they look like, and whether they are worthy of support): "we like the maquis, honneur aux maquis" (236); "the maquis marched down the main street of Culoz, and then everybody stood at attention and sang the Marseillaise, it was interesting to see who out of the population of Culoz were members of the fighting maquis" (237).

The text displays an even more pronounced concern about the visual perception of American soldiers, as Stein expresses a desire to see Allied troops seven times in fifteen pages: "they all also say that in this region there is an English colonel and 15 Canadian officers, but are they, sometimes we believe it and sometimes we do not. If they are here it would be nice to see them" (229); "and now they have just announced on the radio that the Americans are at Grenoble and that is only 80 kilometres away and no opposition in between, oh if they could only come by here. We must see them. There is no way of getting there" (237); "and now if I can only see the Americans come to Culoz I think all this about war will be finished yes I do" (237); "and they say that Americans are at Aix-les-Bains only 25 kilometres away how we want to see them even a little more than the rest of the population which is saying a great deal" (238); "It is very tantalising Americans all over the place . . . and we do not see them, how we want to see them and send word to America and have news from them . . . Dear Americans how we do want to see them" (241); "There are American cars and officers that pass so they say from time to time but I have not seen them and of course seeing is believing" (242); "And now everybody says all the time that American officers are passing through Culoz . . . we are so eagerly waiting to see" (244).

Seeing American soldiers functions as a metonymy for liberation, and this emphatically, excessively expressed desire to see them is accompanied by a final turn in the text toward greater political certainty and a readiness to separate herself from her French neighbors who are less supportive of the Resistance. Stein shows her support of the maquis in an indirect way, describing an argument she has had ("in a loud voice") with a neighbor, a member of "the decayed bourgeoisie, who feel sure that everybody but themselves should be disciplined" (227). This is the first time Stein represents herself in open, assertive disagreement with her French neighbors' political stances, referring, for example, to "the church bigots" who "are all for the Germans" (228). Whereas earlier in the text and in her "Introduction" to Pétain's speeches Stein makes a great point of representing many points of view, here she openly criticizes those who support Germany. In addition, at this point in the text, Stein uses the word "Vichy" for the first time and characterizes it as "the dictatorship or the oligarchy of Vichy" (228). Stein thus offers readers an assertive interpretation of the regime, which up until that point had not even been named in the text, except insofar as it was represented by Pétain, whose name is absent from the narrative's closing pages. Replacing Pétain's unifying "state mask" in the final pages of the text is the visually overwhelming presence of the American G.I.'s, which functions as proof of the German defeat. Here Stein repeatedly states the connection between visual data (seeing the soldiers) and the interpretation or "further facts" associated with that data:

> In the early days when the American army was first passing by . . . the Americans used to say to me but they do not seem to get used to us, we have been right here over a week and they get just as excited when they see us as if they had never seen us before. . . . I said to them you see every time they see you it makes them know it is not a dream that it is true that the Germans are gone. . . . Every time they see you it is a new proof, a new proof that it is all true really true that the Germans are really truly completely and entirely gone, gone gone. (255)

In Stein's postliberation writing, not only do we see a marked turn toward more detailed visual description and a willingness to interpret visual data for readers, but we also see how Stein participates in a militarized gaze, sharing the visual field with the victorious American soldiers. In "Off We All Went to See Germany," published in *Life* in August 1945, the title suggests that the "I" of *Wars I Have Seen* is now part of a larger community of observers with a specific visual goal. However, just as *Wars I Have Seen* immediately runs counter to readerly expectations about the nature of wartime eyewitness narrative by introducing multiple voices and viewpoints, this article immediately swerves from the title's promise: "It was a wonderful experience. And I really pretty well forgot about Germany and the Germans in the enormous pleasure of living intimately with the American Army" (135). As we will see, the central element of Stein's "seeing" Germany is not the visual information she conveys about what she sees there but the way in which she allies herself with the Allied military gaze.

Stein does give a cursory nod to staples of the war-eyewitness genre:

> We hummed along not too high and a beautiful blue sky and we were all looking and soon it was Germany and then John Roessel the navigator came and said here is the Rhine, and there was the dirty Rhine. I had seen

it when I was 19 years old on a vacation and that was long ago. We were all excited and then before we knew it were down in Frankfurt, and hungry. (135)

As in Gellhorn's *A Stricken Field* and in many other wartime and postwar eyewitness narratives, the aerial view of Germany is a desired visual goal,[30] but Stein represents her visual experience by not representing it: she uses the verbal index ("here is the Rhine;" "there was the dirty Rhine;" "soon it was Germany") but provides no description except for the adjective "dirty."

Even when readers assume that Stein is representing a visual experience, they discover a page later that a key element of the scene — the bombarded state of the city — has not yet been mentioned: "Then after considerable conversation, there is always that in the Army, photographing and autographing we had the cars and off we all went to see Germany, we had seen it ruined from the air and now we saw it ruined on the ground. It certainly is ruined, and not so exciting to look at" (136). Stein only mentions the "ruins from the air" after the section of the narrative that describes her viewing them. However, her commitment to verbal representation of visual elements, and to guiding her readers' interpretation of those elements, grows as the text continues:

We drove around and around, everybody had told me that the Germans looked well fed, well yes in a way, but, and eyes trained by four years of occupation, I noticed that the men's clothes did not quite fit them, they were beginning to hang, the women did not yet show anything, the children a little, but as I found out in France, it is men from 30 on who give you the first indication that they are undernourished. Was I pleased to see it, well a little yes. (136)

Here, Stein's description of a visual perception is bound to her own emotional response as she establishes an imaginary dialogue with readers that guides their responses as well. This is one point in the narrative where the "training" Stein's eyes had received by the occupation actually begins to drop away as she not only describes a certain amount of visual data but asserts her own anti-German sentiments in response to that data.

Perhaps just as important as the gradual entrance into fuller interpretation of visual experience is Stein's status as a subject and object of militarized vision in relation to the defeated German populace:

> I had noticed that they turned their heads away and tried not to look at the endless forward and back of the American Army, and then once when we had all gotten out to look at something, I began to realize that they were all looking at Miss Toklas and myself and that some went quite pale and others looked furious. First I was puzzled and then I realized that we were probably the very first ordinary civilian women with American soldiers, not looking official just looking like American women with a group of talking soldiers, and they realized for the first time that there were going to be thousands of civilians coming there just to look as we were looking. After all Germans believe in an army, an army is an army even if it is a conquering army but civilians, just simple civilians, oh dear. (136)

This passage offers several different viewing positions across subject-object and national borders. Like Aldrich just after the Battle of the Marne, Stein is aware of herself, along with Toklas, as a gendered seeing subject and visual object on the militarized visual field. However, while Aldrich is constrained by soldiers from "making a scene" through introducing a resisting or alternative trajectory of vision, Stein's and Toklas's visibility and gaze here participate in and represent a realm of militarized visuality in which civilians, particularly women, reinforce and extend the Allied victory through their status as subjects and objects of sight.

Like Lee Miller and many other journalists just after the fall of the Nazi regime, Stein visited Hitler's retreat at Berchtesgaden, and again like Miller and many of her fellow journalists, Stein's actions at this site display an impulse toward mimetic and iconographic outrage:

> And then we all climbed into our transport, that is our cars and off we went to Hitler. That was exciting. It was exciting to be there . . . and there we were in that big window where Hitler dominated the world a bunch of GI's just gay and happy. It really was the first time I saw our boys really gay and careless . . . while Miss Toklas and I sat comfortably and at home on garden chairs on Hitler's balcony. It was funny it was completely funny it was more than funny it was absurd and yet so natural. We all got to-

gether and pointed as Hitler had pointed but mostly we just sat while they climbed around. (138)

Like Miller taking a nap on Eva Braun's bed and bathing in Hitler's bathtub, Stein and Toklas make themselves "at home" in one of the most powerful symbolic centers of the defeated Third Reich. But while the disturbing power of Miller's act and image comes from her solitary exposure to the interiors of the defeated fascist regime, Stein's relies on a visual and discursive unity with the soldiers: "there we were," getting together as if for a family snapshot, herself and Toklas in the role indulgent parents to "our boys." The group portrait that serves as illustration for the phrase "pointing as Hitler had pointed" published with the article in *Life*, shows Stein and a group of soldiers in profile, standing together on the Berchtesgaden terrace, pointing toward an unseen object (plate 22). Like so many of Stein's wartime utterances, this pose leaves readers in a state of interpretative suspension, as they watch her gesturing emphatically at what they cannot see, pointing toward a significance that is not made explicit. Toward what are Stein and the soldiers pointing? How is the female civilian observer and her readers positioned by and in this photograph?

This group portrait bears comparison with another photograph of a female civilian observer posing with soldiers: Edith Wharton at the French front during World War I (plate 6). Wharton's look, facing toward the viewer and away from the soldiers who peer out at the invisible battleground behind her, both allies her with and separates her from the male military gaze. Her photograph engages her reader in the contradictions of her position as a propagandist for and a resister of militaristic discourse, mapping the simultaneous recuperation and resistance of the female observer's errant looks. Stein's photo creates a very different set of visual trajectories and power relations. Stein allies herself visually not only with the victorious American soldiers but also with the stance of military victory itself. All the figures in the photograph are facing in the same direction, pointing at the same invisible object, miming, Stein claims, the stance with which the leader of the Third Reich "dominated the world" and thereby underscoring the fact of Germany's military defeat.

And yet Hitler's famous gesture, the stiff-armed fascist salute, is modified here, becoming a literal, physical index. Kenneth Burke, in his late

1930's analysis of Hitler's *Mein Kampf,* suggested that the index was a crucial metaphorical presence in fascist ideology. Because the unity of the fascist state depended in part on grouping all "enemies" into the single figure
of "the international Jew," Burke claims, "we have, as unifying step No. 1,
the international devil materialized, in the visible, point-to-able form of
people with a certain kind of 'blood,' a burlesque of contemporary neo-
positivism's ideal of meaning, which insists upon a *material* reference"
(194). What is indexed by fascist ideology is also what is "abjected by" its
"public discourse" (Van Dusen 74): Jewishness, femaleness, homosexual-
ity. By pointing "as Hitler had pointed," Stein might be said to be indexing the "enemy" markers of sexuality and ethnicity that, according to Van
Dusen, she had so successfully "evacuated" from her Pétainist propaganda.
As we have seen in earlier chapters, the index as a sign tends to move in
two directions, both toward and away from the body of the gesturer.

Stein's photograph thus underscores Stein's protected physical presence as an American Jewish lesbian surrounded by American soldiers in
the symbolic center of a regime that persecuted and killed millions of Jews
and homosexuals. Toward the end of the article, she guides her readers' interpretation of the photographs that accompany the article to underline
her and Toklas's safety among the soldiers: "You can see in the photographs
how protectingly they took care of us" ("Off We All Went to See Germany"
141). If the "cubist" composition of World War I replaced the Cartesian
perspectivalist structures of "all previous wars" with their "one man in the
centre surrounded by a lot of other men," the composition of liberation emerging in this photograph appears to be that of a woman in the
center surrounded by a lot of soldiers. Stein reasserts the presence of the
gendered, sexualized, ethnically marked body of the female observer on
the militarized field of vision, but this photograph also suggests that the female observer's vision is effectively absorbed into the trajectory of the military gaze.

Given the body of work produced in the years prior to the publication
of this photograph, I would also suggest that the image is a visual representation of the "liberation" of Gertrude Stein from a set of wartime political loyalties and representations riven by contradictions, doubts, ambiva-
lences and from the continual deferral of political interpretation of visual
and other evidence. The photograph suggests to its viewers that Stein's

shifting, conflicted political stances and her inscriptions of the fragmentation of subjectivity and the constricted visuality of the occupation have — apparently — been resolved or absorbed by the unified, victorious, military gaze. However, Stein's pose, viewed in profile, situates her readers as non-participants on the margins of that gaze, once again deferring a final interpretation, suspended between the Pétainist years behind Stein and the militarized postwar world before her.

Conclusion

THE WOMEN ARTISTS DISCUSSED IN THIS BOOK CON-
structed themselves and their audiences as wartime observers in the face
of a pervasive discourse that depicted female civilians on both European
and American home fronts as particularly prone to political and social manipulation through vision. Before reviewing the difference these women
might make to our understanding of the female gaze during the world
wars, I would like to offer a few more brief parables that suggest the ways
in which that gaze was represented.

George Kennan, U.S. ambassador to Berlin before the entrance of the
United States into World War II, writes of a young French female refugee
returning to her home after the Armistice in 1940:

> I saw a young girl bouncing along on top of one of the carts. Her dress was
> torn and soiled. . . . She was resting her chin in her hand and staring
> fixedly down at the road. All the youth had gone out of her face. There

was only a bitterness too deep for complaint. . . . What would be her re-action to life after this? Just try to tell her of liberalism and democracy, of progress, of ideals, of tradition, of romantic love; see how far you get. Do you think she's going to come out of it a flaming little patriot? She saw the complete moral breakdown and degradation of her own people. She saw them fight each other and stumble over each other in their blind stam-pede to get away and to save their possessions before the advancing Ger-mans. She saw her own soldiers, routed, demoralized, trying to push their way back through the streams of refugees on the highways. She saw her own people pillaging and looting in a veritable orgy of dissolution as they fled before the advancing enemy; possibly she had joined in the looting herself. She saw these French people in all the ugliness of panic, defeat, and demoralization.

The Germans, on the other hand, she saw as disciplined, successful, self-confident. The soldiers were sun-tanned, fit and good humored. She saw them giving food and water to refugees at the crossroads, establishing camps and first-aid stations, transporting the old and the sick in their great Diesel trucks and trailers, guarding against pillaging. What soil here for German propaganda, what thorough plowing for the social revolution which National Socialism carries in its train. (Richler 90)

Kennan's young girl is seen as the representative civilian observer of military defeat, a prime target for Nazi visual propaganda based on her vi-sual experience, a pattern seen in Olivia Manning's World War II novel *The Great Fortune*, which also represents women as duped spectators of Nazi visual manipulation, particularly via sexual desire. The novel's fe-male protagonist is in a Bucharest cinema, "at a matinee, surrounded by women" watching German propaganda films: "Harriet . . . felt they were stunned. Yet, as she left in the crowd, she heard in its appalled whispering a twitter of excitement. One woman said: 'Such beautiful young men!' And another replied: 'They were like the gods of war!'" (qtd. in Richler 60).

In both of these passages, European women are represented as sites of political manipulation and subsequent conquest via the eyes. Kay Boyle's 1944 essay, "Battle of the Sequins," in *Words That Must Somehow Be Said*, provides quite another representation of the female civilian's gaze in rela-tion to the gaze of combatants. Boyle's essay describes a group of women in an American department store, fighting over a limited supply of sequined blouses:

> The women who had gone there to buy were surrounded by mirrors. . . . So that everyone, if he paused for an instant, could see exactly and un-equivocally how he looked. But the faces of these women were turned away, their eyes were fixed on something else; they were there to outwit one another, and they had no time to face themselves. (156)

However, the reflected image that these women refuse to see is not only that of their own faces but that of wounded and dead soldiers:

> Across the walls of the department store there were words written, writ-ten . . . violently and boldly — in spite of their absolute invisibility. . . . "Caution," say these indiscernible words. "You are warned by the author-ities against stopping to look at yourselves in the mirrors." Not because you will see your own shape or face reflected . . . But because the leaves of jungle trees . . . suddenly grow there. . . . And then, without warn-ing, you will come upon the man lying there on the jungle floor with the blood like an open fan, spread as thick as tar and as black, beneath his head. (156–57)

Boyle provides a variation of this scene, again linking the imagined verbal warning of consumer culture against seeing with another image of a seri-ously wounded soldier:

> "Customers are cautioned not to look," says the sign of which no one can perceive the letters, for if you stop to look you will see something you do not wish to see. You will see the shallow water of the river flickering, and out of the muck of the river's bed you will see the other boy crawling on his knees. His shirt is ripped away, and his arm is hanging from the shoul-der by two delicate threads of sinew or nerve or splintered bone, and the blood is not running from it, it is spouting from it the way water will spout from an open water hydrant. (157)

Boyle's essay is most easily read as an indictment of American women's deliberate ignorance and selfish consumerism in the face of the sufferings of soldiers in Europe and Asia. Like the increasingly graphic images of dead American soldiers that the Office of War Information allowed to be published in the last two years of the war, Boyle's verbal representation of the dead and injured soldiers can be seen as "components of a visual environment mobilized to make a distant war seem real to those who were expected to supply the resources, human effort and political support needed for victory" (Roeder 1). However, Boyle's essay also suggests an implicit indictment of several other American wartime visual and verbal discourses: the image-commodity of fashion and consumer culture and the war propaganda effort in the U.S. press. The women engaged in "bitter battle" over "the only size 42 blouse in topaz sequins" and "the topaz-sequined cap to wear with it" (Boyle 155) are experiencing something of the wartime "crisis point in the elaboration of female subjectivity" (Doane 178) created by the ubiquitous image-commodity in women's popular genres, the shortage of luxury goods, women's employment in traditionally male jobs, and the need for rationing and household economies, discussed in chapter 4. While the image-commodity is usually understood as what women look at, the invisible but powerful sign in Boyle's department store is criticized not so much for what it makes women see as for what it turns their gazes away from: a reflecting surface that encompasses both the wartime female seeing subject and the image of the wounded or dead soldier. Moreover, the images of maimed and dead American soldiers from which these female consumers avert their gaze were nowhere near as explicit in the American press photography in 1944 as they are in Boyle's written description. As discussed in chapter 4, photographs containing images of American soldiers' blood did not appear in the U.S. press until 1945, although images of dead American soldiers were published by September 1943, and photographic representations of American soldiers' injuries and deaths grew increasingly explicit during the war's final two years. Boyle's essay, by textually inscribing the extreme injuries that literally could not yet be seen in the American press in 1944, might be understood as an implied criticism of—or a necessary supplement to—an American visual propaganda effort in 1944 that was not making available more explicit photographs of the injured and dead bodies that were at the center of the war.

Another group of images and trajectories of vision appears in Boyle's imagined mirror—that of female combatants in Europe:

In the mirrors there might have been the singular reflection of other women—women who skipped quickly back into a trench before shellfire got them, dragging with them the body of a companion. . . . Perhaps they are Russian women . . . perhaps women of the French maquis. It is difficult to say whether they are beautiful or not, for their faces are masked with filth, with sweat, even with blood. Their skin is cracked, weathered; their nails are not varnished. The dead woman who had fought through three winters with them . . . has been dragged so far by her feet that her mouth and nostrils are stopped with dirt. But whatever has happened to her eyes, the vision is set as clear as glass in them. When this thing is finished, those of them who survive will sit down under a roof again and hold their children against them, and they will never be afraid, no matter how old they grow, to look at their own faces in the mirror. (156)

This passage, so concerned with the relations of the wartime female gaze to consumerism and combat, is reminiscent of the brief glimpse of the women at the lace counter in Edith Wharton's *Fighting France*. There, Wharton's women, despite the fact they are busy "comparing different lengths of Valenciennes," still participate in the uniform, militarized gaze at "France erect on her borders" (39). The women who may not be sharing in that vision are, as we have observed, rendered invisible, a potentially disruptive influence in a text that aims to unify its readers' sympathies behind the French military effort. Boyle's combative shoppers are Wharton's unseen women made visible; they refuse to participate in the unified, militarized gaze that looks at the wounding that results from the war (and supports the military effort that leads to that wounding). The mirror that these women refuse to look at once again establishes the specular ideal we have seen recur throughout the writing of female observers of the world wars: a complete—unequivocal and exact—view not only of the war but also of the seeing wartime subject. This perfectly reflecting specular field seeks not only to contain the gaze of the American female civilian consumer but also to include (and potentially reflects back to that consumer) the specularized gaze of the female combatants: the "vision . . . set as clear as glass" even in the eyes of the dead woman and the self-reflection of the postwar mothers after the imagined Allied victory. Boyle's mirror at least potentially contains a conflicting set of wartime female gazes (the civilian consumer, the war dead and wounded, the surviving, victorious female soldier) in a unifying "singular reflection."

However, the figure of the female civilian as an easily manipulated spectator of visual propaganda through the fascination of sexual attraction or the trauma of having observed military defeat, or as an acquisitive consumer of scarce luxury goods who refuses to "see" the damage done to human bodies by warfare or to participate in the unified gaze required of a successful military effort, constitutes only part of the iconography of the female observer during the world wars. The liminal figure of the female observer on the scene of military engagement; who struggles with the attractions, promises, limitations, difficulties, contradictions, and trauma of wartime visuality; whose gaze is subject to manipulation and control by soldiers; and who is the object of surprised, puzzled, menacing, desiring, or derisive military gaze — this is the figure that emerges in my study, a lightning rod for wartime visual anxieties, inscribing resistances to and gaps in the unifying militarized gaze of a belligerent culture.

Another such observer during this period was the photographer Margaret Bourke-White. The frontispiece of her 1944 collection of photographs and reportage from Italy is a photograph of Bourke-White in a heavy shearling flight suit, standing next to the front end of an airplane. She holds a large camera in one hand and a helmet with goggles in the other. On the first page of text, Bourke-White describes landing on an airstrip in Italy in 1943 to begin an assignment for *Life* magazine and the immediate response of the American ground crew: "'If that ain't an American girl, then I'm seeing things!'" (*Purple Heart Valley* 3). On the following page, Bourke-White describes being "strapped into the observer's seat" aboard a military plane and then reports a dialogue between herself and the American pilot:

> Knowing that one of the functions of observer is to watch all quadrants of the sky for enemy planes, I said to the Captain, "I'm not going to make a very good observer for you. Most of the time I'll have my face buried in my camera, and even when I haven't, I'm not sure I'll know the difference between an enemy fighter and one of ours."
>
> "Don't worry about that," Captain Marinelli said. "If you see any-

thing that looks like an airplane, you tell me and I'll decide whether it's a bandit or an angel." (4)

Bourke-White emphasizes textually and photographically her position, in traditionally male military uniform, as an object of the soldiers' surprised gaze and as an authorized military observer displaying the tools of her trade. Like Wharton and Aldrich, she explicitly represents herself as an inexperienced observer, desiring to "watch all quadrants" of the militarized visual field and ready to have her visual perception interpreted and shaped by the soldier. However, Bourke-White also makes clear that inexperience is not the only hindrance to her status as a "good observer." The camera itself, the instrument of visual representation that authorizes her presence in the military plane in the first place, places a limit on her ability to see according to military regulation.

Bourke-White's time in the observer's seat recalls several of the patterns of gendered visual/power relations we have seen in the work of the other American female observers discussed in this book. These works were produced at different historical moments and different geographical locations during the period of total war that indelibly marks the first half of the twentieth century and were shaped by different aesthetic concerns and political agenda. Nonetheless, all feature visuality — the social, cultural, ideological, and technological forces that help to construct visual experience — as a central element in their representations of the gendered wartime subject.

What we have seen in the preceding chapters is a set of visual and literary texts that address two related problems or issues in the visual cultures of the two world wars: first, the female observer's struggles with the model of the unified subject and with the totalized field of vision that are crucial to militarist discourse and second, the body of the female observer itself as a site of perceptual conflict, with the visual and verbal index often functioning as a sign of that conflict.

Wharton's and Aldrich's work testifies to the immense tensions involved in women's eyewitness propaganda. Both women establish themselves as supporters of a unifying militaristic discourse that would make "disappear" the fact of war's destruction to the human body and that would construct a civilian observer whose literal and figurative line of sight follows the trajectory set by Allied soldiers. However, the very engagement of women's vision tends to break up the unified subject of propaganda and the panoramic visual field with its promise of a complete, consistent view of the war. In these texts, the index points toward two figures that resist representation in wartime propaganda: the wounded or destroyed body of the soldier and the body of the female observer who looks in directions other than those authorized by the closed circuit of soldiers' vision.

When this book turns to World War II, we find several texts that address how fascism, manifested in Nazi policies of torture and genocide, can be understood at least in part as an extreme extension of the totalizing specular structures of militarism. Gellhorn's and Miller's work implicitly rejects the possibility of "seeing all" of the wartime visual field. Instead, they inscribe the limits and failures of seeing in order to emphasize the immense damage done to human bodies by fascism and, in Miller's case, by the war itself. Gellhorn's novel *A Stricken Field* makes clear that under the fascist regime, any attempt at complete visual perception is either thwarted by Nazi expansionism (the arbitrary placing of political borders) or renders vision itself an element of the Nazi torture campaign in occupied Czechoslovakia. The results of this campaign are kept in the forefront of readerly attention through the text's "downcast eyes." However, while the body of the female observer under fascism is subject to surveillance, imprisonment, torture, and execution, *A Stricken Field* also makes possible at least a temporary space in which that body is a site of visual pleasure resistant to specular dangers—the looks shared between Mary Douglas and Rita. Miller's photographs, subverting the totalizing processes of identification with fashion's image/commodity and surrealism's erasure of subject-object boundaries, construct a fragmented, displaced viewer who will support the Allied military effort against the Third Reich while keeping in view the damage done to human bodies by that military effort as well as by the Holocaust. Like Wharton, Miller provides reader-viewers with an image of her own body at the intersection of various wartime gazes. However, the photograph of the former fashion model turned military photographer exposed to and exposing the domestic interiors of the fascist regime does not create complicity between female observer and viewer in resistance to the military gaze, as does Wharton's photograph. Instead, it challenges the viewer's reflex of identification with the image/commodity of fashion discourse, redirecting visual energy toward questions of how the gendered subject is situated in response to the destruction of human bodies under fascism and in the war against fascism.

In its final turn toward two very different World War II home fronts and the work of two very different modernist writers, this book once again addresses the problem of complete, totalized visual perception of war. H.D.'s attempt to construct an expanded field of wartime vision through sustained attention to hallucination, dream-images, and the unrepresentable "something" beyond the borders of normally intelligible visuality asks readers not to reject the possibility of a complete wartime vision (as, I would argue, does the work of Gellhorn and Miller) but rather to reimagine what definitions of "vision" such a totalized field might involve. For H.D., the index gestures toward the imagined extended boundaries of wartime visuality that surround and sustain the female body subject to the menacing gaze of patriarchal visuality and the weaponry of the blitz. Stein's work, in contrast, radically constricts the field of wartime vision. Her Pétainist propaganda and the writing that followed relied not on the possibility, however tenuous, of a panoramic view of the war (such as we see in the work of her friend Aldrich thirty years earlier) but on the suspension of interpretation of visual evidence and the concomitant suspension of political judgment itself for the duration of the war. The image of indexing that closes my chapter on Stein points not only toward Stein's Pétainist politics during the Vichy years and her "liberation" from the conflicts of that position by the unified, victorious American military gaze but also toward the ambivalence and suspended judgments that she attempts to elicit in her wartime readers.

For the women artists discussed in this book, wartime vision always involves conflict and contradiction, and it is inextricably linked to linguistic representation. Its dangerous pleasures (hinted at by H.D.'s women of Chalkis, who speak of the beauty of the gathering Greek forces as well as of the destructive potential of those forces and by Wharton, who acknowledges the "detestable" visual attractions of the French front) readily give way to specular controls and the ruinous effects of militarism and militarism's extreme extensions in fascism. These women do not participate in the wholesale denigration of vision that marks so much of twentieth-century thought but rather inscribe vision as a locus of a struggle, which can never be fully resolved, over the construction and gendering of war-time subjectivity. The term "visual apprehension" itself resonates with both its meanings in the works of the six women I have discussed: their acts of seeing and attempting to understand war — particularly in relation to the gendered subject — necessarily usher in a species of unease that can never be exorcized from sight in a belligerent culture.

NOTES

WORKS CITED

INDEX

Notes

Introduction

1. Some collections that suggest the range of recent scholarship on gender and war are those edited by Cooke and Woollacott; Higonnet et al.; and Elshtain and Tobias. Also see Cooke, *Women and the War Story*; and Raitt and Tate, eds., *Women's Fiction*.

2. A recent example of the continuing critical privileging of the male eyewitness-combatant can be found in several quotations in the first few pages of Hynes's *The Soldiers' Tale*, where veterans of the two world wars claim the visual authority of what Hynes calls "the man-who-was-there": "'How can they judge who have not seen?'"; "'You have to have seen things with your own eyes before you believe them with any intimacy'" (1–2). When Hynes addresses women's narratives of the world wars, he mentions only three narratives concerned with the bombing of cities. Hynes places these narratives within the genre of "The Sufferers' Tale" (223), a genre that includes narratives of prisoners of war, of Holocaust survivors, and of survivors of the atomic bombings at Hiroshima and Nagasaki.

3. Doane outlines a similar contradiction in feminist theorizing about spectatorship in general, especially in film studies:

> although spectatorship is . . . conceptualized in terms which appear to pre-eminently feminize it, feminist film criticism has consistently demonstrated that, in the classical Hollywood cinema, the woman is deprived of a gaze, deprived of subjectivity and repeatedly transformed into the object of a masculine scopophiliac desire. Yet, women would seem to be perfect spectators, culturally positioned as they are outside the arena of history, politics, production — "looking on." (2)

4. Jay also takes up this distinction between passive and active, socially constructed seeing when he writes that observation "could be construed as a . . . complicated interaction of sensations and the shaping or judging capacity of the mind which provided the Gestalt-like structures that made observation more than a purely passive phenomenon" (*Downcast Eyes* 30).

5. Psychoanalytic theorists such as Kaja Silverman draw a distinction between the Lacanian "gaze," a disembodied, unlocalizable "seeingness" that constitutes the subject as always "on view" within the field of vision (168), and the "look," which is "always finite, always embodied" (134). I would like to retain the multiple possibilities of "the gaze" as an embodied, historically specific act of seeing that is subject and resistant to

particular discursive and technological forces. "The gaze" has a rich life outside the precincts of (Lacanian) psychoanalytic theory, although it is there, and later in psycho-analytically based feminist film theory, where it came to prominence. For recent ex-amples of critics working with nonpsychoanalytic definitions of the term, see Bal's "semiotic" definition in "The Gaze in the Closet" (141); and Lutz and Collins's "The Photograph as an Intersection of Gazes."

1. Edith Wharton and the Iconography of War Propaganda

1. See, for example, Gubar's overview of a range of female figures in posters and propaganda leaflets of World War II, 231–40.

2. See Lasswell's pioneering study of World War I propaganda.

3. See, for example, Rupp; Honey; and Gubar on women and propaganda during World War II. On women and World War I propaganda, see Gilbert; and Marcus's "Asylums of Antaeus."

4. According to historians and biographers of women journalists (see Marzolf; Edwards; and Belford), very few women went to France and none to the front lines as credentialed journalists during World War I. However, outside of the official journal-ists' circuit, there was "a rash of 'eyewitness' war-reports by women, ostensibly pub-lished to raise money for various war-efforts" (Tylee 27). See Tylee, chapter 1. Many of the eyewitness reports listed in Tylee's extensive bibliography are postwar narratives written by nurses and ambulance drivers; see Marcus's "Corpus/Corps/Corpse" for a discussion of the liminal, textual, and physical spaces occupied by these women dur-ing World War I.

5. See Schwartz (21–31 and 55–56); Douglass; and Quirk on Bergson's influence on Modernist poetics.

6. Also see Cobley 6–7.

7. For a brief survey of Western traditions of ocularcentrism and its construction of subjectivity, see Keller and Grontkowski; Irigaray's work has become crucial and of-ten controversial in discussions of what Nancy K. Miller calls "the politics of visibility in the formation of sexual identity" (*Subject to Change* 164).

8. The impulse to strike a truce in the war between image and text is a feature of much recent critical theory in several disciplines that analyze the intersections and interplay of visual and linguistic representation. See, for example, Mitchell, *Iconology*; Bal; J. Miller; Melville and Readings; and Birdsell and Groarke.

9. That the political loyalties of a collective subject are more readily engaged through images is apparent to a 1918 admirer and interpreter of Allied war-posters:

> It has been the duty of all the graphic artists of all the countries . . . to launch the strongest possible appeal for unity of purpose and activity against a com-mon foe. . . . this campaign of graphic propaganda has registered a marked effect upon the minds of millions of people who understand most easily a message that has been conveyed to them through the medium of the eye.

The average person is more likely to believe what he sees than to believe what he hears. (Hamilton 47)

10. See Peirce, 106; as well as Mitchell (*Iconology* 56–60); and Steiner (19–22) for discussions of Peirce's semiotic theories. Also see Krauss, "Notes on the Index" (parts 1 and 2) in *The Originality of the Avant-Garde* for a discussion of the index in 1970's visual art.

11. See Wiltsher's *Most Dangerous Women* on feminist pacifists during the Great War; and Marcus, "Asylums of Antaeus," on the British suffrage movement's use of posters.

2. Mapping the Female Observer in *A Hilltop on the Marne*

1. Aldrich's letters to Stein and Toklas are in the Yale Collection of American Literature Beinecke Rare Book and Manuscript Library, Yale University.

2. The painter Bill Sullivan claims that "Panorama in Western art seems to come from a need to portray battles — a place large enough for armies to heroically engage with a grandeur befitting the occasion — a visual epic" (qtd. in Clark 21).

3. Wallach makes a similar point in his study of nineteenth-century American landscape painting: "In the panorama, the world is presented as a form of totality; nothing seems hidden; the spectator, looking down upon a vast scene from its center, appears to preside over all visibility" (83).

4. This model of the inclusive, authentic war-panorama also extended to journals that combined visual image and text. *Le Panorama de la Guerre*, published in France from 1914 to 1919, consisted of a series of captioned photos of trench life, diplomatic meetings, and military parades (much like the images distributed by the American press). It promised to provide the reader/viewer with "a collection of living, exact, and precise documents" that would enable the war to "unroll before our eyes, day by day, almost hour by hour" (1; my translation). The presence of such a journal suggests that French civilians experienced a sense of visual loss or lag similar to the one felt by "neutral" Americans in 1915. Virilio claims that during World War I, "*Direct vision was now a thing of the past*: . . . the target area had become a cinema 'location,' the battlefield a film set out of bounds to civilians" (11).

5. See Bryson ("The Gaze" 88); Steiner (*Colors of Rhetoric* 180); and Jay ("Scopic Regimes" 7) for discussions of the viewer in classical perspective.

6. Also see Emanuelli (7).

7. The bulk of Crary's study examines a variety of nineteenth-century prephotographic "optical devices" that were involved in this process of regulation.

8. By referring to the already outmoded art form of the panorama (Lawson and Crary both claim that the panorama lost its popularity by the 1890s), Aldrich's text is also able to gesture toward this earlier visual mode, one particularly popular in France, of understanding war. Lawson points out that the panoramic painting "The Siege of

Paris," which depicted the 1870 German invasion of Paris during the Franco-Prussian War and "which stood in the Champs-Elysées through the 1870's and into the '80's," was one of the most popular panoramas of the nineteenth century (90).

9. Schweik sees the closely connected figures of the female reader and the female spectator of war as essential to (literary) wartime discourses (90). Also see Marrinan's discussion of how Napoleonic history-painting evoked both a "viewer" and a "reader" (187–88, 191).

10. "Panoramic" photographs of World War I battlefields, complete with typed place-names and dotted lines or hand-drawn arrows superimposed on the photographs and indicating sites of specific military actions, were a common feature of postwar guidebooks to the battlefields of France. See, for example, the 1919 guidebook, *The Americans in the Great War*, that contains a photograph captioned "Panoramic view of St. Mihiel and the valley of the Meuse seen from the top of Paroches fort" (62–63). Like the panoramic photograph in *Hilltop*, the photographs in this guidebook are taken from enough of a distance that the dotted indicator lines appear to point at no identifiable place but rather at a particular set of pixels — an index reminiscent of the sailor's pointing toward unidentified smudges meant to represent the act of military destruction of human bodies in the Brangwyn posters discussed in chapter 1.

11. See Barthes 38–41.

12. Benstock reads this passage of "Patriarchal Poetry" as an exemplar of what she calls "Expatriate Modernism" ("Expatriate Modernism" 32–34).

3. A *Stricken Field* and the Field of Vision:
Fascism, Gender, and the Specular

1. See Doenecke for a discussion of American interventionist and anti-interventionist organizations and rhetoric in 1940–41.

2. On the Nazi party's use of visual art, see *Assault on the Arts*; Barry; and Adam.

3. This is also the case with much of Gellhorn's wartime journalism: her pronoun shifts often make it impossible to draw strict boundaries around the identities of character, reader, and writer or around soldiers, civilians, and military observers. See her reports in *Collier's*, listed in Rollyson's bibliography, many of which are reproduced in *The Face of War* and *The View from the Ground*.

4. As the title and subtitle of his recent book suggests, Jay uses the figure of "downcast eyes" to represent "the denigration of vision in twentieth-century French thought." I want again to emphasize, as I have in my Introduction, that for Gellhorn, as for the other artists whose work is studied here, what is "denigrated" is not vision itself but the particular and heavily gender-inflected tradition of specularity that constructs a totalized visual field.

5. The difficulties of representing fascism's victims as seeing subjects is worked out not only in the text's treatments of Rita's visual experiences of torture but also in a

brief parable-like section of chapter 7 that is narrated from the point of view of an elderly blind woman from the Sudetenland living in a refugee camp outside Prague.

6. See Bridenthal, Grossman, and Kaplan; and Koonz for an analysis of the construction of womanhood during the Third Reich.

4. Vision, Violence, and *Vogue:*
War and Correspondence in Lee Miller's Photography

1. See Penrose, *The Lives of Lee Miller.*

2. The most often cited sources regarding this aspect of surrealism are André Breton and Max Ernst. Breton claims that in a surrealist universe, "life and death, the real and the imaginary, the communicable and the incommunicable, high and low [will] cease to be perceived as contradictions" (123). Ernst writes that the goal of surrealist art is "the coupling of two realities, irreconcilable in appearance, upon a plane which apparently does not suit them" (13).

3. For other critiques of the surrealist construction of women in visual art, see Chadwick, chapter 1; and Kuenzli.

4. See "Mimicry and Legendary Psychasthenia."

5. Scarry uses metaphors of vision quite consistently in her study of the language used to describe war in *The Body in Pain.* Scarry tends to conflate language and seeing, using metaphors of visibility to describe linguistic acts: to speak or write about something is to make it "visible" (13). What I would like to do here is to focus, as it were, on actual visual representations of the wartime body in pain and the dead body, to problematize, and then to examine the conflicts and contradictions involved in the act of making war visible through photography.

6. For other studies of the construction of wartime female subjectivity through government propaganda in the United States, see Honey; Rupp; Michel; Milkman; and Gubar.

7. Doane uses the opening sequence from the 1945 Max Ophuls film *Caught* as an example of such a process. The screen is filled with a series of close-ups in which a woman's hands turn the pages of a fashion magazine, and two female voice-overs discuss their desire for the jewelry and clothing pictured in the photographs and drawings. For another study of how fashion magazines construct female subjectivity, see Rabine, who examines how, since the late 1960s, publications like *Vogue* have functioned both as instruments of consumer capitalism and "forums for North American feminism" (59). The essays in Benstock and Ferriss's *On Fashion* represent a range of emerging critical discourses on gender and fashion.

8. Miller's political explanation of the state of French fashions should also be read as part of a larger effort on the part of the French and American press to manage the crisis of perception that emerged when it became clear that most of the large Parisian fashion houses had remained open and productive under German occupation and that so many resources had been used to continue to produce *haute couture* under the oc-

cupation's constrained economic conditions. According to Taylor, after the Allies' first view of post-Liberation fashion, "there were whispers of collaboration, and the fate of the huge French fashion industry hung in the balance" (135). Miller's description of the anti-German qualities of the clothing and hairstyles is very similar to that offered by the French designer Lucien Lelong in the December 1944 issue of *Vogue*: "every yard of fabric wasted in France was seen as a yard less of fabric that could be sent to Germany" (qtd. in Taylor 136).

9. Many, and some of the most powerful, of Miller's photographs taken during the war were never published in *Vogue*, and many have only recently become available through the Lee Miller Archives in Sussex; and through the publication of *Lee Miller's War*; and Penrose's; and Livingston's (*Lee Miller: Photographer*) illustrated biographies. (Krauss and Livingston also include reproductions of several Miller photographs in the bibliography/biography section of *L'Amour Fou*; as do Chadwick; and Stich.) These photographs' rejection by *Vogue* editors is, perhaps, as telling about the magazine's construction of its wartime female audience and about Miller's self-construction as an observer of war as are those accepted for publication. I am interested in Miller as an artist and in the audience her photographs imagined as well as actually addressed.

10. Bryson has articulated an important distinction between "the gaze" and "the glance." See *Vision and Painting* 93; and Caws 119.

11. See Roeder, chapter 1; and Moeller 224–227.

12. See Bryson, *Vision and Painting* 87–88.

13. Abzug writes that this kind of reaction was widespread among American soldiers who liberated the camps. See especially chapters 1 and 7.

14. A typical issue of *Vogue* from this two-year period runs approximately 200 pages. There are generally 100 or so pages of full-page advertisements placed before the table of contents in each issue. Of the approximately 100 pages left, another 80 or so are occupied by more full-page advertisements, 10 by full-page features, and 10 by a continuation of the features' text, usually a single column placed between two columns of smaller advertisements. Of the features, generally three quarters are devoted to fashion developments.

15. Miller's description of these domestic spaces and consumer objects is part of a larger pattern in American reportage on the end of the Third Reich. For example, Hamburger's "Letter from Berchtesgaden" in the June 9, 1945, issue of the *New Yorker* describes a visit to Hitler's Berchtesgaden retreat in advertising terms: "The Fuhrer's bathroom . . . has green tiled walls, in the best *Good Housekeeping* tradition. . . . some rooms [are] right out of an ad for Men of Distinction" (499–500).

5. Visual Disturbances in an Expanded Field: H.D. and the Blitz

1. H.D. claims in the "Writing on the Wall" section of *Tribute to Freud* that "war, its cause and effects, with its inevitable aftermath of neurotic breakdown and related nerve disorders" was "the thing I primarily wanted to fight in the open" in her analysis with Freud in the 1930s (93).

2. Dates are from Friedman's "H.D. Chronology" (53–54).

3. Two critics of H.D.'s work touch on different areas of the terrain I am trying to explore here. Friedman writes that in *The Gift* "[t]he politics of fascism are super-imposed onto the psychodynamics of the patriarchal family" (*Penelope's Web* 339), and Hirsch observes "in several prose works written by 'H.D.' in the forties and fifties" there is "an obsession with problems of seeing and their relation to the constitution of sub-jectivity" (438). This chapter's concerns might be said to be located at the intersection of Friedman's and Hirsch's statements, as it traces how the female seeing subject is con-structed (and constructs herself) in relation to militarist and patriarchal visuality.

4. In *Notes on Thought and Vision* (composed 1919), H.D. describes another set of contrasting, simultaneous modes of vision: "vision of the womb and vision of the brain" (20), which DuPlessis suggests correspond to "sexual energy" and "psychic understanding" (40). H.D. also refers to these two modes as "lenses": "the love-mind and the over-mind are two lenses. When these lenses are properly adjusted, focused, they bring the world of vision into consciousness. The two work separately, perceive separately, yet make one picture" (23). Morris ("The Concept of Projection" 279–80); and DuPlessis (41) suggest these "lenses" are devised in response to the lenses of H.D.'s astronomer father and biologist grandfather, whom this chapter will also discuss. Edmunds tropes a somewhat different duality in H.D.'s work as two bodies: "One oc-cupies the space of epiphany. . . . The other occupies the space of narrative or history, a body containing pain and contained by plot" (1).

5. Bryson uses the term "expanded field" to define the radically decentered model of visuality and subjectivity in the work of the philosopher Keiji Nishitani ("The Gaze" 87–88, 97–101). Krauss uses the phrase "expanded field" in reference to a logi-cal structure known as a Klein group that problematizes a set of binary oppositions ("Sculpture in the Expanded Field" 37–38).

6. For other readings of the relation between the Sartrean and Lacanian gaze, see Melville, "Division of the Gaze;" and Silverman 164–170.

7. Jay, for example, imagines Sartre's symbolic park as a "universe of . . . warring gazes" and claims that for Lacan, "vision . . . may be understood as a conflictual field in which the looker is always a body to be observed" (*Downcast Eyes* 289, 368). Silver-man characterizes Sartre's account of the visual field as "'personalistic,' a kind of fight to the death of looks" (166).

8. Following Mulvey's "Visual Pleasure and Narrative Cinema," feminist film critics have dealt extensively with the issue of the dominating, potentially menacing "male gaze" and have explored how the female seeing subject is constructed by and re-sponds to the "technologies of gender" (deLauretis 1) operating in cinema and in the larger visual realm. See, for example, deLauretis; Kaplan; Pribram; and Doane.

9. Silverman also theorizes an "ethics of the look" (170) by positing what she calls a "productive look" that would "challenge . . . the complacencies of the self and the limitations of the given-to-be-seen" (193).

10. In her introduction to "H.D. by Delia Alton," Morris demonstrates the diffi-

culty involved in precisely identifying what kind of visual field H.D. is attempting to represent; she writes that H.D.'s work constitutes a "visionary quest for an idea or an ideal, a messenger or visitor from another realm of consciousness, another field of vision or knowledge" (177). Edmunds names this element in H.D.'s work an "equation between the manifestations of the unconscious and those of eternity" (89).

11. Sword notes that a "prophetic, visionary stance" is a traditional means of gaining "poetic authority" (1) and sees H.D.'s World War II poetry as part of her attempt to "define and affirm the poet's role as an interpreter . . . of visionary consciousness" (171). DuPlessis suggests that H.D. "reclaimed various non-secular spaces of prophecy, of vision" in part as a "*sub rosa* critique of Freud" (83). Also see Schweik's reading of Muriel Rukeyser's allusion to Saint Bernadette in the 1944 poem, "Letter to the Front" as an assertion that "the source of the healing spring, of true vision in wartime, may be imagined as a woman" (157).

12. Edmunds and Morris ("Signaling") both address the vexed question of the possible political functions of H.D.'s visionary method. Morris observes that feminist readers of H.D. "tend to mute the mysticism of H.D.'s practice" (qtd. in Edmunds 89), and Edmunds reminds feminist critics that "H.D.'s visionary resolutions, which held a literal, practical value for her, cannot be implemented in a political sphere defined in secular and historical terms" (qtd. in Edmunds 89). However, both critics find that H.D.'s more mystically inflected work has some "rhetorical purchase" (Edmunds 89) in the secular, historical sphere. Edmunds suggests that the "ostensibly ahistorical order of maternal plenitude" that H.D. inscribes in her wartime poem *Trilogy* "derives its redemptive status from its ascribed power to represent badly needed resolutions to current historical conflicts or problems" (90). Morris writes that "although in isolation this practice [of divination and prophecy] may seem apolitical or even antipolitical, when used to readjust or confirm social relations, mysticism overlaps with politics" (qtd. in Edmunds 197n. 153).

13. Bryson observes that one of the limitations of Lacan's theory of the Gaze is its focus on "the genetic and formative moment, not the long and diverse elaborations of adult life" ("The Gaze" 105). Edmunds notes that Melanie Klein, whose theories of female aggression Edmunds believes influenced H.D., also tended to focus on an infant's "unconscious phantasies" to the exclusion of what Klein's daughter Melitta Schmideberg called "'the patient's actual environment and reality situation'" (qtd. in Edmunds 197n. 155). Edmunds suggests that "H.D. may have been familiar with this line of critique" (197n. 155) because she underwent analysis with Klein's son-in-law, Walter Schmideberg, who broke away from Kleinian psychoanalysis in favor of a more orthodox Freudian approach (26–27).

In discussing the role of vision in *The Gift*, Hirsch focuses on the early stages of subject development represented there, suggesting that "scenes of 'wounding' are linked to the mysteries of copulation, childbirth, and death, so that seeing itself becomes a kind of wounding, a trauma of initiation" (438). I would argue that *The Gift* also inscribes an expanded field of vision based on the "elaborations of adult life" in response to these scenes of wounding.

14. Unless otherwise indicated, quotations from *The Gift* are taken from the New Directions edition, which is a significantly shortened version of the text of the typescript in the Beinecke Library. As indicated, other quotations are taken from the unaltered versions of chapters of *The Gift* published separately: "Dark Room" (*Montemora* 8 [1981]); and "The Dream" (*Contemporary Literature* 10 [autumn 1969]).

15. In the final chapter of *The Gift*, the narrator makes explicit the connection between this opening parable of the burning girl and the blitz: "I could visualize the very worst terrors, I could see myself caught in the fall of bricks, and I would be pinned down under a great beam, helpless. Many had been. I would be burned to death. . . . I could think in terms of one girl in a crinoline, I could not visualize civilization other than a Christmas tree that had caught fire" (136).

16. A later chapter of *The Gift* rewrites this parable, leaving the interpretation of the significance of the mother's tears to Hilda and her mother. The narrator tells a story of a neighborhood boy, Teddie Kent, who had fallen out of a tree and broken his arm.

> And [his brother] Jack Kent ran away and was gone a whole night, and when
> he came back Mrs. Kent cried, and that seemed a funny thing to do. "Why
> did she cry, Mama?"
> "Well, she cried with relief, because she was so happy."
> "Can one cry because one is happy, Mama?" (72)

This alternative parable of two brothers answers the father's parable with two female interpreters, dialogically deciding on the motive for crying. The chapter title in which this rewritten parable appears, "Because One is Happy," underlines the importance of this parable, the way that a mother-daughter dialogue can reinterpret tears, the visible maternal response to a son's danger.

See Huston's "Tales of War and Tears of Women" for a discussion of the cultural status and sign-systems of women's tears in war-narrative.

17. Bryson claims that Sartre's field of vision "is restricted to its twin poles of subject and object . . . as though the watcher in the park and the intruder . . . were supplied with optical frames—binoculars, telescopes, viewfinders—which restrict . . . the surrounding world to just these two poles" ("The Gaze" 96).

18. For an analysis of writing about women's war-related insanity during and after World War I, see Marcus, "Asylums of Antaeus." For a discussion of H.D.'s fiction about World War I and its relation to "civilian war neuroses," see Tate, "HD's War Neurotics."

19. Friedman writes that the father's telescope and the grandfather's microscope are both "phallic metonyms for their (masculine) knowledge, [and] are inseparable from their status as professors in society and patriarchs in the family" (*Penelope's Web* 335).

20. See Conley for a discussion of Lacan's theory of how "the letter inspires a subject to fix his or her relation to visibility through the coagulation of indeterminate impressions" (51).

21. Friedman also observes that "H.D.'s play with the presence/absence in the water drop resonates with contemporary Lacanian theory of the word or signifier as a material presence that signifies the absence of the phallus" (*Penelope's Web* 405n. 46).

In one reading, this contemplation of the letter *O* as both a visual and lexical sign is a paradigmatic modernist moment; even more specifically, a paradigmatic imagist moment. Morris observes that Imagist theory looked toward the ideal of conflating visual and verbal orders of meaning, of valorizing the "word-thing," a "direct, visibly concrete, natural rather than conventional . . . picture language" ("The Concept of Projection" 276). For Rose, "the modernist stress on the purity of the visual signifier easily dissolves into an almost mystic contemplation" (230). Such a modernist moment in H.D.'s wartime writing actually turns the "mystic contemplation" of the letter-image into a political visual act, interrogating the specular codes of sexual difference implicit in patriarchal visuality, the strict difference between "something" and "nothing." This particular modernist instance of "mystic contemplation" and visual disturbance might be read as an illustration of Rose's claim that "there can be no work on the image, no challenge to its powers of illusion and address, which does not simultaneously challenge the fact of sexual difference" (226).

22. Schweik reads this review as part of H.D.'s critique of the passive or helpless female spectator of violence (252).

23. Mandel briefly refers to this passage in connection to H.D.'s work with film in the 1930s (316).

24. That H.D. positions her seeing subject on a border that gestures beyond normal intelligible visuality is suggested by *Webster's* definition of "hinterland" as "the land or district behind that bordering on a coast or river; inland region."

25. Silverman has a definition of the "screen" similar to Bryson's: "that repertoire of ideologically marked representations through which the members of a particular culture are visually defined and differentiated from one another" (244n. 22).

26. Similar images appear in the first section of *Trilogy*, "The Walls Do Not Fall," composed in 1942:

the bone-frame was made for
no such shock knit within terror,
yet the skeleton stood up to it

. . . .

yet the frame held   (*Collected Poems* 510–11)

6. Occupation and Observer: Gertrude Stein in Vichy France

1. Chessman writes that "Stein encourages her 'public' . . . to engage in reading as a process filled with starts and stops, moments of confusion or uncertainty" (8). Marianne DeKoven suggests that Stein's experimental writing "obstruct[s] normal read-

ing, . . . preventing us from interpreting the writing to form coherent, single, whole, closed, ordered, finite, sensible meanings" (qtd. in Chessman 10–11).

2. See Kedward, *Resistance in Vichy France* 16.

3. See, for example, Wagner-Martin 246; Mellow 445–46; and Sprigge 236. Two biographers, Bridgman and Hobhouse, also cite Stein's friend, the painter Francis Rose, who was "amorously involved with . . . Nazi leaders" and claimed in his memoir to have "extracted a promise from Goering to watch over Gertrude Stein and Alice in France" (Hobhouse 218). How much did Stein's and Toklas's "internal exclusion" (Benstock, "Paris Lesbianism" 339) differentiate their position from that of other American citizens in Vichy and occupied France? Historians offer differing assessments: Paxton writes that "[t]he most fortunate foreigners escaped from French law by holding a favored passport: British or American" (371), while Sweets claims that "after the American and British landings in North Africa in 1942, Vichy ordered strict surveillance over the activities of British and American citizens, and early in 1943 26 of the 206 British and American adults living in the region of the Auvergne were sent to camps in Northern France" (103).

4. Mellow, citing *The Alice B. Toklas Cookbook*, writes that Toklas gave an acquaintance sheets of gelatin she used to make a dessert, but that only "later . . . learned he had needed it for making false papers" (442).

5. However, histories of the Resistance movement indicate that at the time when Stein was composing "The Winner Loses"—the months following the signing of the Armistice in summer 1940—the rural-based Maquis movement barely existed and would not gain any substantial presence in the French countryside for another two years: "Resistance movements of 1940–42 were urban-based . . . , and the idea of guerrilla warfare in the countryside or even a tactical retreat into the hills had hardly been discussed" (Kedward, "The Maquis and the Culture of the Outlaw" 233).

6. Resistance to the STO provided the basis for the growth of the Maquis in the last two years of the war, as many of the young men who fled to mountain hiding places took up arms in active resistance to the German occupation forces (Kedward, "The Maquis and the Culture of the Outlaw" 233).

7. Sweets attempts in his work to caution readers "who would see the history of wartime France in clear shades of black and white—the good resisters versus the bad collaborators. To sort out the threads of heroism, treason, good, and evil is exceedingly difficult. In wartime France, everything was complicated" (111–12). Sweets's words recall Stein's own postwar statement that "living in an occupied country is very complicated" (qtd. in Bridgman 335).

8. There is, again, some divergent opinion among historians about when Pétain began to experience a decline in popularity. Paxton writes that Pétain "could still be cheered in Nancy, Rouen, and even in Paris in the spring of 1944" (326), suggesting that "[t]he presence of Pétain, the World War I victor, the cautious hoarder of French blood, the bulwark against revolution, the wise father, provided moral cover for the regime long after all its other members had been widely discredited" (236). Sweets, however,

claims that "undeniable signs of hostility to the regime and even to the Marshal were apparent much sooner than has often been acknowledged" (146).

9. He cites as an example the journal *Combat*, which "could not bring itself to mount a full denunciation of Pétain until May 1942" (*Resistance in Vichy France* 145). Even those statements about Pétain that anticollaborationist writers characterized as "clear" were ambivalent: in December 1941, a *Combat* editorial stated, "Our attitude to the Marshal is clear. In him are two men. The man of World War I whom we respect and the man of collaboration whom we refuse to follow" (qtd. in Kedward, *Resistance in Vichy France* 146).

10. The historian H. R. Kedward writes that the 1936 legislative elections in France indicate that the Ain was one of the "majority right-wing *départements*" of what became the Southern Zone (*In Search of the Maquis* 153–54).

11. According to Paxton, "[t]he conditions of life in both zones of France declined from austerity in 1940 to severe want in 1944. . . . The main concern was food. France was eventually the worst nourished of the western occupied nations" (237–38).

12. While many biographers (see Wagner-Martin 246–47; Mellow 445; Sprigge 234; Bridgman 317) have mentioned Stein's translation project, the first sustained critical reading of the "Introduction" is Van Dusen's in *Modernism/Modernity*, which has also published the "Introduction," the typescript of which is in Columbia University's Butler Library. Page numbers for the "Introduction" refer to the text as it appears in *Modernism/Modernity*.

13. Stein's address to American readers also ran against one current of mainstream French feeling about the United States at this point in the war. According to Paxton, "The United States, . . . supplier of food and possible arbiter to end the war, lost some of its appeal to neutralist French opinion after it also became a belligerent in December 1941" (240).

14. According to Kedward, it was not until July 1941 that *Libération* first "firmly established the synonymity of Vichy and collaboration" (*Resistance in Vichy France* 138).

15. However, even while acknowledging Pétain's favor with the greater part of French citizens at this point in the war, Sweets maintains that Pétain's speeches themselves were somewhat less acclaimed. Sweets quotes a government official based in Clermont-Ferrand who wrote in May 1941—less than a year after the Vichy government was formed—that "'the public no longer attaches any significance to speeches. It would like a break from them, preferring action'" (145).

16. Van Dusen makes a case for the unity of the subject that Stein inscribes in the "Introduction's" opening paragraphs, claiming that the text erases markers of ethnicity and sexuality in favor of nationality:

> The multiplicity of Stein as a subject is reduced to participation in nationality via the evacuation of her affiliation with a threatened ethnicity and her practice of lesbian sexuality. . . . The "Introduction" attempts to achieve [an] . . . "impossible impermeability" of the subject by evacuating Stein's

gender, her lesbianism, and her Jewishness. . . . Without these markers, the unified self presented by Stein can be safely subsumed in the dominant category of "we in France." (74)

17. Van Dusen claims that "[t]hrough a series of adverbial repetitions, Stein creates a sense of the inevitable: 'always,' 'gradually,' 'then,' 'day after day,' 'little by little,' 'more and more'" and notes that "the term used by Pétain on 20 June 1940 to justify his arrangement with Germany to the French is 'inescapable' ('*inéluctable*')" (71–72).

18. Kedward notes that "the Vichy France of that second winter of Occupation is far from showing the homogeneous respect for the Pétain regime which so many writers observed in 1940" (*Resistance in Vichy France* 150).

19. Given that the passage was written in late 1941 or early 1942, before the massive roundups and deportations of Jews from both zones of France in the spring and summer of 1942, a reader might infer that Stein is referring primarily to the leftist political figures of the Popular Front who governed France in the late 1930s, before the defeat and occupation. Van Dusen suggests that this group also includes Jews, Marxists, and bourgeois democrats (79), as these groups were subject to severe persecution within France well before the deportations to German concentration camps of mid-1942. See Marrus and Paxton, *Vichy France and the Jews*, for a detailed account of Vichy's virulently anti-Semitic policies, beginning as early as July 1940, just a month after the defeat of the French army, with the *Statut des Juifs* that immediately established employment quotas for Jews in certain professions ("medicine, law, dentistry, pharmacy, journalism, theater, and film" [Kedward, *Resistance in Vichy France* 166]); denied any employment for Jews in government posts, armed services, or state education; and allowed regional departments "to intern all foreign Jews in 'special camps'" (Kedward, *Resistance in Vichy France* 166).

20. For example, the secretary of education in the early years of the Vichy regime, Jérôme Carcopino, spoke of Pétain as the man "'who, alone among so many, from 1914 to 1918, had acquired enough glory to win the admiration of the victors, to stop the invasion of 1940, and whose presence at the head of the government symbolizes and guarantees the unity of France and its empire'" (qtd. in Sweets 46).

21. In her 1940 article "The Winner Loses," Stein represents without any opposition an attitude shared by many French citizens after the signing of the Armistice: "they said they are very pleased . . . they were tired of the weak vices that they were all indulging in . . . and they all think that French people were getting soft, and French people should not be soft" (636–37; also see Paxton 23).

22. Paxton writes that "Vichy veterans had every incentive to produce a flood of selective, self-justifying prose to show that in 1940 they had already seen the world in 1944 terms" (45).

23. See Wagner-Martin 135–41.

24. Well before World War II, Stein proved to be concerned with the problem of war and visual representation and how representations of war play an important role in

the construction of the seeing subject. This is most evident in her 1935 lecture, "Pictures," published in *Lectures in America*. For the most part, "Pictures" is composed of a series of autobiographical parables of Stein's installment as an observer on the field of vision, particularly in relation to painting. The first three of these parables are explicitly connected to the problem of looking at representation of battles and at battlefields themselves. At issue in the piece is not only Stein's preoccupation with questions of "resemblance" (the relationship between representation and what is represented) but also the observer's early formation by military representation and history—concerns to which Stein returns in *Wars I Have Seen*.

25. If the events that Stein is describing took place during or after the summer of 1942, it is possible that Gilbert and his wife had been deported in one of the massive roundups of Jews and other "undesirables" that were taking place across France at the instigation of the German occupying forces and carried out by French police and pro-fascist militia groups. It is also possible that Gilbert had been sent to Germany under the STO or that he had become a *réfractaire*, hiding in the surrounding mountains to escape the forced-labor program.

26. See Paxton 294.

27. Wagner-Martin notes that for Stein and Toklas, "[p]assing as older French-women might have been possible if they had not had to speak. . . . Gertrude's voice was harshly American—and she would never remember to lower it to avoid a soldier's over-hearing" (241).

28. For the majority of French people during the Vichy period, as for Stein, the word "deportation" usually referred to the removal of non-Jewish French citizens under the forced labor program of the STO and not the deportation of Jews to the camps in Germany and Poland: "The program of labor conscription for Germany . . . came to seem the real deportation, and . . . distracted attention from the journeys to Auschwitz" (Paxton 184).

29. Paxton claims that many "solid citizens" along with members of the armed Resistance who came from formal military backgrounds, tended to view the maquis as "brigands" or "anarchists" (293) and that "in 1944 . . . the overwhelming majority of Frenchmen, however they longed to lift the German yoke, did not want to lift it by fire and sword" (294–95).

30. Another example is found on the opening pages of Bourke-White's 1946 collection of photographs and essays on the defeated Germany, *Dear Fatherland, Rest Quietly* (1).

Works Cited

Abzug, Robert H. *Inside the Vicious Heart: Americans and the Liberation of Nazi Concentration Camps*. New York: Oxford UP, 1985.

Adam, Peter. *Art of the Third Reich*. New York: Abrams, 1992.

Aldrich, Mildred. *A Hilltop on the Marne: Being Letters Written June 3–September 8, 1914*. Boston: Houghton, 1915.

The Americans in the Great War. Vol. 2. Clermont-Ferrand, France: Michelin, 1919.

Assault on the Arts: Culture and Politics in Nazi Germany. New York: New York Public Library, 1993.

Bal, Mieke. "The Gaze in the Closet." Brennan and Jay 139–53.

———. "His Master's Eye." *Modernity and the Hegemony of Vision*. Ed. David Michael Levin. Berkeley: U of California P, 1993. 379–404.

———. "Visual Poetics: Reading with the Other Art." *Theory Between the Disciplines: Authority/Vision/Politics*. Ed. Martin Kreiswirth and Mark A. Cheetham. Ann Arbor: U of Michigan P, 1990. 135–50.

Barry, Stephanie. *"Degenerate Art": The Fate of the Avant-Garde in Nazi Germany*. New York: Abrams, 1991.

Barthes, Roland. *Image, Music, Text*. Tr. Stephen Heath. New York: Farrar, Straus, Giroux, 1977.

Belford, Barbara. *Brilliant Bylines: A Biographical Anthology of Notable Newspaper Women in America*. New York: Columbia UP, 1986.

Benstock, Shari. "Expatriate Modernism: Writing on the Cultural Rim." *Women's Writing in Exile*. Ed. Mary Lynn Broe and Angela Ingram. Chapel Hill: U of North Carolina P, 1989. 19–40.

———. "Paris Lesbianism and the Politics of Reaction, 1900–1940." *Hidden from History*. Ed. Martin Duberman, Martha Vinicus, and George Chauncey, Jr. New York: New American Library, 1989. 332–46.

Benstock, Shari, and Suzanne Ferriss, eds. *On Fashion*. New Brunswick: Rutgers UP, 1994.

Berman, Russell. *Modern Culture and Critical Theory: Art, Politics, and the Legacy of the Frankfurt School*. Madison: U of Wisconsin P, 1989.

Birdsell, David, and Leo Groarke. "Toward a Theory of Visual Argument." *Argumentation and Advocacy* 33 (summer 1996): 1–10.

Bourke-White, Margaret. *Dear Fatherland, Rest Quietly*. New York: Simon, 1946.

———. *They Called It Purple Heart Valley: A Combat Chronicle of the War in Italy*. New York: Simon, 1944.

Bowen, Barbara E. *Gender in the Theater of War: Shakespeare's Troilus and Cressida.* New York: Garland, 1993.

Boyle, Kay. "Battle of the Sequins." *Words That Must Somehow Be Said: Selected Essays of Kay Boyle, 1927–1984.* Ed. Elizabeth Bell. San Francisco: North Point, 1985. 155–58.

Brennan, Teresa, and Martin Jay, eds. *Vision in Context.* New York: Routledge, 1996.

Breton, André. *Manifestoes of Surrealism.* Tr. Richard Seaver and Helen Lane. Ann Arbor: U of Michigan P, 1971.

Bridenthal, Renata, Atina Grossman, and Marion Kaplan, eds. *When Biology Became Destiny: Women in Weimar and Nazi Germany.* New York: Monthly Review, 1984.

Bridgman, Richard. *Gertrude Stein in Pieces.* New York: Oxford UP, 1970.

Bryson, Norman. "The Gaze in the Expanded Field." Foster 86–108.

———. *Vision and Painting: The Logic of the Gaze.* New Haven: Yale UP, 1983.

Buitenhuis, Peter. *The Great War of Words: British, American, and Canadian Propaganda and the Great War, 1914–1933.* Vancouver: U of British Columbia P, 1987.

Burke, Kenneth. "The Rhetoric of Hitler's 'Battle.'" *The Philosophy of Literary Form.* U of California P, 1941. 191–220.

Caillois, Roger. "Mimicry and Legendary Psychasthenia." Tr. John Shepley. *October* 31 (Winter 1984): 17–32.

Calder, Angus. *The People's War: Britain, 1939–1945.* New York: Pantheon, 1969.

Caws, Mary Ann. *The Art of Interference: Stressed Readings in Verbal and Visual Texts.* Princeton, NJ: Princeton UP, 1989.

Chadwick, Whitney. *Women Artists and the Surrealist Movement.* Boston: Little, 1985.

Chessman, Harriet. *The Public Is Invited to Dance: Representation, the Body, and Dialogue in Gertrude Stein.* Stanford, CA: Stanford UP, 1989.

Civil War Photographs. Advertisement. *Review of Reviews* September 1914: 6.

Clark, Marcia, ed. *The World Is Round: Contemporary Panoramas.* Trevor Park-on-Hudson, NY: Hudson River Museum, 1987.

Cobley, Evelyn. *Representing War: Form and Ideology in First World War Narratives.* Toronto: U of Toronto P, 1993.

Conley, Tom. "The Wit of the Letter: Holbein's Lacan." Brennan and Jay 45–61.

Cooke, Miriam. *Women and the War Story.* Berkeley: U of California P, 1996.

Cooke, Miriam, and Angela Woollacott, eds. *Gendering War Talk.* Princeton, NJ: Princeton UP, 1993.

Crary, Jonathan. *Techniques of the Observer: On Vision and Modernity in the Nineteenth Century.* Cambridge: MIT, 1990.

DeKoven, Marianne. *A Different Language: Gertrude Stein's Experimental Writing.* Madison: U of Wisconsin P, 1983.

———. *Rich and Strange: Gender, History, Modernism.* Princeton, NJ: Princeton UP, 1991.

deLauretis, Teresa. *Technologies of Gender.* Bloomington: Indiana UP, 1987.

Doane, Mary Anne. *The Desire to Desire: The Woman's Film of the 1940's.* Bloomington: Indiana UP, 1987.

Doenecke, Justus D. *In Danger Undaunted: The Anti-Interventionist Movement of 1940–1941 as Revealed in the Papers of the America First Committee.* Stanford, CA: Hoover Institution Press, 1990.

Douglass, Paul. *Bergson, Eliot, and American Literature.* Lexington: UP of Kentucky, 1986.

DuPlessis, Rachel Blau. *H.D.: The Career of That Struggle.* Bloomington: Indiana UP, 1986.

Edmunds, Susan. *Out of Line: History, Psychoanalysis, and Montage in H.D.'s Long Poems.* Stanford: Stanford UP, 1994.

Edwards, Julia. *Women of the World: The Great Foreign Correspondents.* Boston: Houghton, 1988.

Elsaesser, Thomas. "Primary Identification and the Historical Subject." *Narrative, Apparatus, Ideology: A Film Theory Reader.* Ed. Philip Rosen. New York: Columbia UP, 1986.

Elshtain, Jean Bethke, and Sheila Tobias, eds. *Women, Militarism, and War: Essays in History, Politics, and Social Theory.* Savage, MD: Rowman and Littlefield, 1990.

Emanuelli, Sharon. Foreword. Clark 1–7.

Ernst, Max. *Max Ernst: Beyond Painting and Other Writings by the Artist and His Friends.* New York: Wittenborn, Schultz, 1948.

Flanner, Janet. *Pétain: The Old Man of France.* New York: Simon, 1944.

Foster, Hal, ed. *Vision and Visuality.* Seattle, WA: Bay Press, 1988.

Friedman, Susan Stanford. "H.D. Chronology: Composition and Publication of Volumes." *Sagetrieb* 6 (fall 1987): 51–55.

———. *Penelope's Web: Gender, Modernity, and H.D.'s Fiction.* New York: Cambridge UP, 1990.

Friedman, Susan Stanford, and Rachel Blau DuPlessis, eds. *Signets: Reading H.D.* Madison: U of Wisconsin P, 1990.

Gandelman, Claude. *Reading Pictures, Viewing Texts.* Bloomington: Indiana UP, 1990.

Gasché, Rodolphe. *The Tain of the Mirror: Derrida and the Philosophy of Reflection.* Cambridge, MA: Harvard UP, 1986.

Gellhorn, Martha. *The Face of War.* New York: Atlantic Monthly, 1988.

———. *A Stricken Field.* 1940. New York: Penguin, 1986.

———. *The View from the Ground.* New York: Atlantic Monthly, 1988.

Gilbert, Sandra. "Soldier's Heart: Literary Men, Literary Women, and the Great War." Higonnet et al. 197–226.

Gubar, Susan. "'This Is My Rifle, This Is My Gun': World War II and the Blitz on Women." Higonnet et al. 227–59.

Hamburger, Philip. "Letter from Berchtesgaden." *The New Yorker Book of War Pieces.* New York: Schocken, 1988. 497–501.

Hamilton, Clayton. "Posters for the Great War: How the Artists of America and the Allied Nations Have Served the Cause of Civilization with Their Stirring Appeals to Patriotism." *Munsey's Magazine* 64 (June–September 1918): 38–57.

H.D. *Collected Poems, 1912–1944.* Ed. Louis L. Marz. New York: New Directions, 1983.

———. "Dark Room." *Montemora* 8 (1981): 57–76.

———. "The Dream." *Contemporary Literature* 10 (Autumn 1969): 605–26.

———. *The Gift*. New York: New Directions, 1982.

———. *Notes on Thought and Vision*. San Francisco: City Lights, 1982.

———. *Palimpsest*. 1926. Carbondale: Southern Illinois UP, 1986.

———. Review of "The Passion and Death of a Saint." *Close Up* 3 (July 1928): 15, 23. Reprinted in *The Gender of Modernism*. Ed. Bonnie Kime Scott. Bloomington: Indiana UP, 1990. 129–33.

———. *Tribute to Freud*. New York: New Directions, 1956.

———. *Within the Walls*. Iowa City: Windhover Press, 1993.

Higonnet, Margaret Randolph, and Patrice L.-R. Higonnet. "The Double Helix." Higonnet et al. 31–47.

Higonnet, Margaret, Jane Jenson, Sonya Michel, and Margaret Collins Weitz, eds. *Behind the Lines: Gender and the Two World Wars*. New Haven: Yale UP, 1987.

Hirsch, Elizabeth A. "Imaginary Images: 'H.D.,' Modernism, and the Psychoanalysis of Seeing." Friedman and DuPlessis 430–51.

Hobhouse, Janet. *Everybody Who Was Anybody: A Biography of Gertrude Stein*. New York: Doubleday, 1977.

Honey, Maureen. *Creating Rosie the Riveter: Class, Gender, and Propaganda During World War II*. Amherst: U of Massachusetts P, 1984.

Huston, Nancy. "Tales of War and Tears of Women." *Women's Studies International Forum* 5.3/4 (1982): 271–82.

Hynes, Samuel. *The Soldiers' Tale: Bearing Witness to Modern War*. New York: Penguin, 1997.

Irigaray, Luce. *Speculum of the Other Woman*. Tr. Gillian C. Gill. Ithaca: Cornell UP, 1985.

Jacobus, Mary. *Reading Woman*. New York: Columbia UP, 1986.

James, William. *The Principles of Psychology*. 1890. Cambridge, MA: Harvard UP, 1981.

Jay, Martin. *Downcast Eyes: The Denigration of Vision in Twentieth-Century French Thought*. Berkeley: U of California P, 1993.

———. "The Rise of Hermeneutics and the Crisis of Ocularcentrism." *The Rhetoric of Interpretation and the Interpretation of Rhetoric*. Ed. Paul Hernadi. Durham, NC: Duke UP, 1989. 55–74.

———. "Scopic Regimes of Modernity." Foster 2–25.

Kaplan, E. Ann. *Women and Film: Both Sides of the Camera*. New York: Methuen, 1983.

Kedward, H. R. Foreword. Proud v–vi.

———. *In Search of the Maquis: Rural Resistance in Southern France, 1942–1944*. New York: Oxford, 1993.

———. "The Maquis and the Culture of the Outlaw." Kedward and Austin 232–51.

———. *Resistance in Vichy France: A Study of Ideas and Motivation in the Southern Zone, 1940–1942*. Oxford: Oxford UP, 1978.

Kedward, H. R., and Roger Austin. Introduction. Kedward and Austin 1–10.

————, eds. *Vichy France and the Resistance: Culture and Ideology.* Totowa, NJ: Barnes and Noble, 1985.

Keller, Evelyn Fox, and Christine R. Grontkowski. "The Mind's Eye." *Discovering Reality: Feminist Perspectives on Epistemology, Metaphysics, Methodology, and the Philosophy of Science.* Ed. Sandra Harding and Merrill B. Hintikka. Boston: D. Reidel, 1983. 207–24.

Koonz, Claudia. *Mothers in the Fatherland: Women, the Family, and Nazi Politics.* New York: St. Martin's, 1987.

Krauss, Rosalind. "Corpus Delicti." Krauss and Livingston 55–112.

————. *The Originality of the Avant-Garde and Other Modernist Myths.* Cambridge: MIT, 1985.

————. "Sculpture in the Expanded Field." *The Anti-Aesthetic: Essays on Postmodern Culture.* Ed. Hal Foster. Port Townsend, WA: Bay Press, 1983.

Krauss, Rosalind, and Jane Livingston. *L'Amour Fou: Photography and Surrealism.* New York: Abbeville, 1985.

Kuenzli, Rudolf E. "Surrealism and Misogyny," *Surrealism and Women.* Ed. Mary Ann Caws, Rudolf Kuenzli, and Gwen Raeberg. Cambridge: MIT, 1991. 17–25.

Lacan, Jacques. *The Four Fundamental Concepts of Psycho-analysis.* Ed. Jacques-Alain Miller. Tr. Alan Sheridan. New York: Norton, 1978.

Lasswell, Harold. *Propaganda Technique in the World War.* New York: Knopf, 1927.

Lawson, Thomas. "Time Bandits, Space Vampires." *Artforum* 26 (1988): 88–95.

Leed, Eric. *No Man's Land: Combat and Identity in World War I.* New York: Cambridge UP, 1979.

Le Panorama de la Guerre 1 (February 1915).

Livingston, Jane. *Lee Miller: Photographer.* New York: Thames and Hudson, 1989.

————. "Man Ray and Surrealist Photography." Krauss and Livingston 113–52.

Lutz, Catherine, and Jane Collins. "The Photograph as an Intersection of Gazes: The Example of *National Geographic.*" *Visualizing Theory: Selected Essays from V.A.R., 1990–1994.* Ed. Lucien Taylor. New York: Routledge, 1994.

Mandel, Charlotte. "Magical Lenses: Poet's Vision Beyond the Naked Eye." *H.D.: Woman and Poet.* Ed. Michael King. Orono, ME: National Poetry Foundation, 1986.

Marcus, Jane. "The Asylums of Antaeus: Women, War, and Madness: Is There a Feminist Fetishism?" *The Difference Within: Feminism and Critical Theory.* Ed. Elizabeth Meese and Alice Parker. Amsterdam: Benjamins, 1989. 49–83.

————. "Corpus/Corps/Corpse: Writing the Body in/at War." *Arms and the Woman: War, Gender, and Literary Representation.* Ed. Helen M. Cooper, Adrienne Munich, and Susan Squier. Chapel Hill: U of North Carolina P, 1989. 124–67.

Marrinan, Michael. "Literal/Literary/'Lexie': History, Text, and Authority in Napoleonic Painting." *Word and Image* 7 (1991): 177–200.

Marrus, Michael, and Robert O. Paxton. *Vichy France and the Jews.* New York: Basic Books, 1981.

Marzolf, Marion. *Up from the Footnote: A History of Women Journalists*. New York: Hastingshouse, 1977.

Mellow, James. *Charmed Circle: Gertrude Stein and Company*. New York: Praeger, 1974.

Melville, Stephen. "Division of the Gaze, or, Remarks on the Color and Tenor of Contemporary 'Theory.'" Brennan and Jay 101–16.

Melville, Stephen, and Bill Readings, eds. *Vision and Textuality*. Durham, NC: Duke UP, 1995.

Michel, Sonya. "American Women and the Discourse of the Democratic Family in World War II." Higonnet et al. 154–67.

Milkman, Ruth. "American Women and Industrial Unionism During World War II." Higonnet et al. 168–81.

Miller, J. Hillis. *Illustration*. Cambridge, MA: Harvard UP, 1992.

Miller, Lee. "Believe It." *Vogue*, June 1945: 104–7.

———. *Lee Miller's War*. Ed. Antony Penrose. Boston: Little, 1992.

———. "Paris." *Vogue*, November 1944: 95–99 ff.

———. "U.S.A. Tent Hospital." *Vogue*, September 1944: 138–43 ff.

Miller, Nancy K. *Subject to Change: Reading Feminist Writing*. New York: Columbia UP, 1988.

Mitchell, W. J. T. *Iconology: Image, Text, Ideology*. Chicago: U of Chicago P, 1986.

———. *Picture Theory*. Chicago: U of Chicago P, 1994.

Mizejewski, Linda. *Divine Decadence: Fascism, Female Spectacle, and the Makings of Sally Bowles*. Princeton, NJ: Princeton UP, 1992.

Moeller, Susan. *Shooting War: Photography and the American Experience of Combat*. New York: Basic, 1989.

Moi, Toril. *Sexual/Textual Politics: Feminist Literary Theory*. New York: Methuen, 1985.

Morris, Adalaide. "The Concept of Projection: H.D.'s Visionary Powers." Friedman and DuPlessis 273–96.

———. Introduction. "H.D. by Delia Alton." *Iowa Review* 16 (fall 1986): 174–78.

———. "Signaling: Feminism, Politics, and Mysticism in H.D.'s War Trilogy." *Sagetrieb* 9 (Winter 1990): 121–34.

Mould, David. *American Newsfilm, 1914–1919: The Underexposed War*. New York: Garland, 1983.

Mulvey, Laura. "Visual Pleasure and Narrative Cinema." *Screen* 16 (Autumn 1975): 6–18. Reprinted in *Visual and Other Pleasures*. Bloomington: Indiana UP, 1989. 14–26.

Paxton, Robert O. *Vichy France: Old Guard and New Order, 1940–1944*. 1972. New York: Columbia UP, 1982.

Peirce, C. S. "Logic as Semiotic: The Theory of Signs." *Philosophic Writings of Peirce*. New York: Dover, 1955.

Penrose, Antony. *The Lives of Lee Miller*. New York: Holt, 1985.

Perloff, Marjorie. "Six Stein Styles in Search of a Reader." *A Gertrude Stein Companion*. Ed. Bruce Kellner. New York: Greenwood, 1988.

Pétain, Henri Philippe. *Paroles aux Français: Messages et Ecrits*. Lyon: H. Lardanchet, 1941.

Pickering, Robert. "Writing under Vichy: Ambiguity and Literary Imagination in the Non-occupied Zone." Kedward and Austin 260–64.

Pribram, Deirdre. *Female Spectators: Looking at Film and Television*. New York: Verso, 1988.

Proud, Judith. *Children and Propaganda: Il Etait une Fois . . . Fiction and Fantasy in Vichy France*. Oxford: Intellect, 1995.

Quirk, Tom. *Bergson and American Culture: The Worlds of Willa Cather and Wallace Stevens*. Chapel Hill: U of North Carolina P, 1990.

Rabine, Leslie W. "A Woman's Two Bodies: Fashion Magazines, Consumerism, and Feminism." Benstock and Ferriss 59–75.

Raitt, Suzanne, and Trudi Tate, eds. *Women's Fiction and the Great War*. New York: Oxford, 1997.

Richler, Mordecai, ed. *Writers on World War II: An Anthology*. New York: Vintage, 1991.

Roeder, George H. *The Censored War: American Visual Experience During World War Two*. New Haven: Yale UP, 1993.

Rollyson, Carl. *Nothing Ever Happens to the Brave: The Story of Martha Gellhorn*. New York: St. Martin's, 1990.

Rose, Jacqueline. *Sexuality in the Field of Vision*. New York: Verso, 1986.

Ruddick, Sara. *Maternal Thinking: Toward a Politics of Peace*. New York: Ballantine, 1989.

Rupp, Leila J. *Mobilizing Women for War: German and American Propaganda, 1939–1945*. Princeton, NJ: Princeton UP, 1978.

Russo, Mary. "Female Grotesques: Carnival and Theory." *Feminist Studies/Critical Studies*. Ed. Teresa deLauretis. Bloomington: Indiana UP, 1986. 213–29.

Sartre, Jean-Paul. *Being and Nothingness*. Tr. Hazel E. Barnes. New York: Philosophical Library, 1956.

Scarry, Elaine. *The Body in Pain: The Making and Unmaking of the World*. New York: Oxford UP, 1985.

Schiffman, Winifred. "Artist Biographies and Bibliographies," Krauss and Livingston 191–237.

Schnapp, Jeffrey T. "Epic Demonstrations: Fascist Modernity and the 1932 Exhibition of the Fascist Revolution." *Fascism, Aesthetics, and Culture*. Ed. Richard J. Golsan. Hanover, NH: UP of New England, 1992. 1–37.

Schwartz, Sanford. *The Matrix of Modernism: Pound, Eliot, and Early Twentieth-Century Thought*. Princeton, NJ: Princeton UP, 1985.

Schweik, Susan. *A Gulf So Deeply Cut: American Women Poets and the Second World War*. Madison: U of Wisconsin P, 1991.

Silverman, Kaja. *The Threshold of the Visible World*. New York: Routledge, 1996.

Sprigge, Elizabeth. *Gertrude Stein: Her Life and Work*. New York: Harper, 1957.

Stein, Gertrude. "Introduction to the Speeches of Maréchal Pétain" (1942). *Modernism/Modernity* 3.3 (September 1996): 93–96.

————. "Mildred Aldrich Saturday." Ts. Gertrude Stein Papers. Beinecke Library, Yale U, New Haven, CT.

————. "Off We All Went to See Germany." *Life*. August 6, 1945. Reprinted in *How Writing Is Written*. Ed. Robert Haas. Los Angeles: Black Sparrow, 1974.

————. *Paris France*. 1940. New York: Liveright, 1970.

————. "Picasso." *Picasso: The Complete Writings*. Ed. Leon Katz and Edward Burns. New York: Liveright, 1970. 19–88.

————. "Pictures." *Lectures in America*. 1935. Boston: Beacon Press, 1985. 59–90.

————. "A Transatlantic Interview 1946." *The Gender of Modernism*. Ed. Bonnie Kime Scott. Bloomington: Indiana UP, 1990. 502–16.

————. *Wars I Have Seen*. New York: Random House, 1945.

————. "The Winner Loses: A Portrait of Occupied France." 1940. *Selected Writings of Gertrude Stein*. Ed. Carl Van Vechten. New York: Random House, 1946.

Steiner, Wendy. *The Colors of Rhetoric: Problems in the Relation Between Modern Literature and Painting*. Chicago: U of Chicago P, 1982.

Stich, Sidra. *Anxious Visions: Surrealist Art*. New York: Abbeville Press, 1990.

Sweets, John. *Choices in Vichy France: The French under Nazi Occupation*. New York: Oxford UP, 1986.

Sword, Helen. *Engendering Inspiration*. Ann Arbor: U of Michigan P, 1996.

Tate, Trudi. "HD's War Neurotics." Raitt and Tate 239–62.

Taylor, Lou. "Paris Couture, 1940–1944." *Chic Thrills: A Fashion Reader*. Ed. Juliet Ash and Elizabeth Wilson. New York: Harper, 1992.

Theweleit, Klaus. "The Bomb's Womb and the Genders of War (War Goes on Preventing Women from Becoming the Mothers of Invention)." Cooke and Woollacott 283–315.

————. *Male Fantasies*. Vol. 1 of *Women, Floods, Bodies, Histories*. Tr. Stephen Conway. Minneapolis: U of Minnesota P, 1989.

Townsend, Janis. "Mildred Aldrich." Vol. 1 of *American Women Writers: A Critical Reference Guide from Colonial Times to the Present*. Ed. Lina Mainiero. 4 vols. New York: Ungar, 1979. 36–38.

Tylee, Claire. *The Great War and Women's Consciousness: Images of Militarism and Womanhood in Women's Writings, 1914–1964*. Iowa City: U of Iowa P, 1990.

Van Dusen, Wanda. "Portrait of a National Fetish: Gertrude Stein's Introduction to the Speeches of Maréchal Pétain." *Modernism/Modernity* 3.3 (September 1996): 69–92.

Virilio, Paul. *War and Cinema: The Logistics of Perception*. Tr. Patrick Camiller. New York: Verso, 1989.

Wagner-Martin, Linda. *Favored Strangers: Gertrude Stein and Her Family*. New Brunswick: Rutgers UP, 1995.

Wald, Priscilla. *Constituting Americans*. Durham, NC: Duke UP, 1995.

Wallach, Allan. "Making a Picture of the View from Mount Holyoke." *American Iconology*. Ed. David Miller. New Haven: Yale UP, 1993. 80–91.

Wharton, Edith. *Fighting France: From Dunkirk to Belfort*. New York: Scribner's, 1915.

————. "Writing a War Story." Vol. 1 of *The Collected Short Stories of Edith Wharton*. 2 vols. Ed. R. W. B. Lewis. New York: Scribner's, 1968. 359–70.

White, Hayden. "The Value of Narrativity in the Representation of Reality." *On Narrative*. Ed. W. J. T. Mitchell. Chicago: U of Chicago P, 1981.

Wiltsher, Anne. *Most Dangerous Women: Feminist Peace Campaigners of the Great War*. Boston: Pandora, 1985.

Index

Jean Gallagher is an assistant professor of English in the Department of Humanities and Social Sciences at Polytechnic University in New York City. She has published articles in *LIT: Literature, Interpretation, Theory*; *Commonweal*; and the *American Book Review*. She is currently working on a manuscript dealing with gender, modernism, and visual culture.